Reparations
Fleecing America

By

James J. Dobranich Sr.

ISBN: 1-4107-3766-7 (e-book)
ISBN: 1-4107-3765-9 (Paperback)

This book is printed on acid free paper.

1stBooks - rev. 07/23/03

To my parents now deceased
Joseph and Mary Dobranich
And to my Wife, Edith
For her help in the
Preparation of this book

Introduction

A group of Black lawyers are planning to initiate a joint—class action lawsuit—primarily directed at the white citizens and corporations of this country, to pay reparations to the descendants of our nations past slaves; slaves that were first enslaved by their African Brothers and later sold into the world wide slave markets. That history shows that the origin of slavery can be traced back to the nations of Africa has no bearing on the matter—it is only the White mans money that they are interested in. To them, I would like to quote an old axiom: "As you sow, so shall you reap."

This lawsuit, as I understand it, will be against the white race at large—disregarding the reality that neither you nor any of your present day family or ancestors had anything to do with slavery—slavery at anytime or of any kind! However, this is a class action scheme—pitting one class of citizens against the other. Why? To enrich themselves at the expense of race relations and national unity.

This action, if initiated, will soon become a racially motivated disaster. In short it will soon prove to be nothing but an out and out attempt to fleece the pockets of the white-man. Without a doubt, such an action would soon find our races being split further apart instead of coming together. It seems, as of late, a group of "shyster lawyers" are hell bent on enriching themselves, not for Justice but for personal, selfish and unscrupulous financial gain. They must not succeed! If they were successful in achieving their goal, there would be no end to it.

From time to time, and down through the ages people have been entwined in some form of bondage that they had to overcome. You, my black friends have not been alone. You must not allow the sacrifices of your ancestors to be denigrated in such unscrupulous endeavors. The sacrifices made by your ancestors enabled you, their decedents, to live in the greatest country on the face of this planet—the United States of America.

We the citizens of this nation of all races, creeds and colors have and must continue to live together in harmony—to do otherwise would be catastrophic. Do not be swayed by a few "Gold-Diggers."

"People hate those who make them feel their own inferiority." Lord Chesterfield.

Chapter I

Racial Pride

In every race, creed and color It can be found that among each race there are good people as well as bad. Still, the majority of people, throughout the races, are honest, hard working, productive members of our society.

However, as of late, I find the white race being singled out by the black leadership, as the reason for the ills and failures of the blacks. It is hard to listen to some members of the black race who continually blame the white race as if they were the only race of people to have participated in the slave trade.

It is time that the white man repudiates such accusations. We are a great race of people! The white race has, as no other race of people on the face of this planet, contributed as much to the other races of people or countries in there advancement and to the betterment of all mankind. It is those of the white race who can stand tall and with their heads held high!

If one was willing to look, and in fairness, they would find the white race in the forefront of social progress. Progress that improved life for the betterment of all.

It is the citizens from other countries that are flocking to our shores. Why? To either escape their countries governments or to look for a better way of life. It is true that the blacks were originally introduced into the Americas as slaves. However, it is also true that they were Introduced to this continent, long before the United States became a nation.

This country established nation status in I776 and in the year I808, prohibited the Importation of slaves; thus becoming one of the first nations to initiate positive action to end slavery within their country. From our nations founding, it only took our forefathers 32 years too curtail the importation of slaves to our shores.

It is historically documented that people of the white race were the founders of this nation. It was the Pilgrims, the English Religious Puritans, who founded the colony of

Plymouth Massachusetts in I620. Further attesting as to whom, in fact, were the founders of this nation is the following:

1. It was 56 white men, our founding fathers, who signed the Declaration of Independence.
2. It was the Revolutionary Army, under the command of George Washington that fought and won our nations independence. With few exceptions, this army was composed of white men.
3. It was George Washington that became our nations first president. As such, he is considered the "Father of our Country."

It was the people, primarily of the white race, who came together from all points of our planet that put aside their differences and joined together in "Unity," to build our country. They became a nation of citizens that joined together to achieve common goals and objectives. They were a "Melting Pot" of humanity, putting aside their differences, their petty or personal grievances.   In this vein, they worked together, suffered numerous hardships and defended their country, when it became necessary, as only true patriots would. They did not look back but always looked ahead. They became "We the People in order to form a more perfect Union..." It was the coming together of our people—not diversity—that made this country great?   In this manner they, our forefathers—the pioneers, the explorers, the settlers—who went on before us to settle the land and build this great nation.

Today we are unmatched in time, in place and throughout history in respect to our nations high status as the most desirable nation to live in. This, while some black people who have the privilege of living in this country, cannot seem to stop blaming and complaining. A few will also admit that they feel no allegiance to this nation or its flag!

The citizens of this nation have lived through the times of Civil War, the great Depression, and World Wars II and I and, in each case, we brought honor and glory to our people and our nation. Time after time we have been tested and time after time we have endured. As Americans and to the amazement of the world at large—we have exceeded beyond all expectations.

The majority of the white race is a self reliant, imaginative and hard working people; willing to accept full responsibility for their actions. As such, we should never accept unfounded personal attacks on our race, our flag or our country. Those that came to this land, such as my father, were willing to work within the system—they expected and got no special consideration. They, my father and the likes of him paid honor to this country and appreciated what it could do for them. They accepted the opportunity to stand or fall on their own merits— never asking for "affirmative action or special assistance." Sure many of them fell by the wayside however, they had the gumption to get back on their feet and try and try again. They were not quitters—nor were they crybabies or willing to play the blame game. They were their own man! They did not bite the hand that fed them.

Still, there are amongst us, those who cry out for more and more government largess and control. Yes, for government "freebees" they are willing to run down our country our citizens. Yes, they are quick to run down the whites of this nation but slow to look at their faults. In this day and age, it seems that only the white man is to be held responsible for their past misdeeds and mistakes.

Recently, I received a copy of comments made, several years ago, by Gordon Sinclair, of Canadian television. What follows is the full text of his trenchant remarks as printed in the United States Congressional Record. (Note: These comments, with minor updating, could be applied to our country to almost any period of time in our nations history):

> "This Canadian thinks it is time to speak up for the Americans as the most generous and possible the least appreciated people on all the earth. Germany, Japan and, to a lesser extent, Britain and Italy were lifted out of the debris of war by the Americans who pored in billions of dollars and forgave other billions in debts. None of these

countries is today paying even the interest on its remaining debts to the United States.

When the franc was in danger of collapsing in l956, it was Americans who propped it up, and their reward was to be insulted and swindled on the streets of Paris. I was there. I saw it. When earthquakes hit distant cities, it is the United States that hurries to help. This spring, 59 American communities were flattened by tornadoes. Nobody helped.

The Marshall Plan and the Truman Policy pumped billions of dollars into discouraged countries. Now newspapers in those countries are writing about the decadent, war mongering Americans. I would like to see just one of this countries that is gloating over the erosion of the United States build its own airplane. Does any other country in the world have a plane equal to the Boeing Jumbo Jet, the Lockheed Tri-Star, or the Douglas 10, if so, why don't they fly them?

Why do International lines except Russian fly American Planes?

Why does no other land on earth even consider putting a man or women on the moon?

You talk about Japanese Technocracy, and you get radio. You talk about German Technocracy, and you get automobiles.

You talk about American Technocracy, and you find man on the moon—not once but several times—and safely home again.

You talk about scandals, and the Americans put theirs right in the store window for everyone to look at. Even their Draft Dodgers are not pursued and hounded. They are here in our streets, and most of them are, unless they are breaking Canadian laws, getting dollars from Ma and Pa at home to spend here.

When the railways of France, Germany and India were breaking down through the ages, it was Americans who rebuilt them. When the Pennsylvania Railroad and the New York Central went broke, nobody loaned them even an old caboose. Both are still broke.

I can name you 500 times when the Americans raced to the help of others in trouble. Can you name me even one time when anyone else raced to the Americans in trouble?

Our neighbors have faced it alone, and I'm one Canadian who is damned tired of hearing them get kicked around. They will come out of this thing and with their flag high. And when they do, they that are entitled to thumb their nose at the lands that are gloating over their present troubles. I hope Canada is not one of them."
Stand Proud America.

I will, as my Canadian friend said, always stand proud of my country. Yes and to those who would have but one intent—that is to take over or overthrow this country—I would willingly fight and die to maintain my countries heritage and all that it stands for and entails—without question or hesitation.

"Who saves his country, saves himself, saves all things and all things saved do bless him! Who Let's his country die, lets all things die, dies himself ignobly and all things dying curse him."
Benjamin H. Hill.

Chapter II

Race and affinity for Africa

In their Book "Africa-Africans" by Paul Bohannan and Phillip Curtin it was noted: "Race, as Concept," is that it is based, in fact, on two concepts, which are: 1. Race has become the idiom in which it has cast some of its practices of and ideas about persecution and 2. Moreover, it has been utilized as a technical term by biological sciences and particularly, by genetics. Thus it has been assumed by the Western World that the popular idiom and the scientific concept has some bearing on each other."

Race, a social problem, is what might be called cultural displacements. Actually, the whole Race question, in biological science, is a group of organisms that the members of which "Statistically" become significant, when the proportion of their genes is reached for the purposes of scientists, to resolve problems relative to race. However, by gene counting there is no point relative in nature at which one race can become another by virtue of having more or less genes common to a race. Race is part of the analytical process of sciences, not part of the data. Basically we are all, biologically speaking—alike!

Further, races are the consequences of interbreeding populations. As such they must meet in order to breed. Races must have a geographical dimension: is area in which it is represented—simply stated—by interbreeding populations. As the interbreeding of present day races occurs, with the breaking down of geographical and social barriers, new geographical isolation or new social barriers again create new interbreeding populations, a new set of races may result. Today, we are seeing more and more interracial breeding among/between the races now living in this land of ours.

However, in the modern world, as defined in the dictionary, race also means something else—that is: Race is derived from the Latin term for "root" and also, it has been used in English to refer to sex (the female race), to humanity (the human race) and additionally to refer to members of nationalities, religions and so on! In the United States, of late, race is the revolutionary cry with which new standards of equality and justice are being demanded, such as quotas, affirmative action and such.

In the United States, the many monumental social changes that followed the Civil War, gave rise to many of the present day beliefs about race in America. Not until after the Civil War, between the states, is it that social Problems that existed for centuries are, only now, being expressed in an idiom of "race." Still there is no clear line that can be indisputable drawn that, Unequivocally, can show that one group is Caucasoid and the other Negroid. Still, we are making race judgments primarily based on the color of ones skin and yes, not by the content of there Character.

Until the 1770s, or so, in the Americas, more Africans by way of the slave trade, were received than its total number of immigrants from Europe. This was particularly true within the nations of Brazil, the Caribbean and the Southern Americas. In these regions/countries and ultimately in Europe as well, Negro skin color, hair texture and facial features were associated with the status of slavery. Prejudices based on cultures and social rank were blended together and expressed as "racial prejudices." As a consequence the basis of skin color came to be adopted, only in North America but also in a major part of the world, before this land was established as a nation. In view of this, it can rightly be stated that racial prejudices were well established, before our nation was established. It should also be noted that the classifications of "Human beings" by skin color goes back to the Ancient Egyptians, even though the concept of "Race" does not.

In America, throughout the debates about the abolition of the slave trade, in the eighteen Hundreds, similarities between Caucasians and Negroes were minimized to the most basic by the Christians. The Christians claimed that Africans were "fellow creatures." However, a few would care to deny such an inconsequential claim. Many arguments proceeded on rather or not the "Savages" were "naturally" inferior. As a consequence, the stereotypes of the "Negro" began to appear in the great chain of being, of which echoes were still being heard well into the Twentieth Century. Unfortunately, in some areas of the country, they still exist.

> "Prejudices are rarely overcome by argument; not being founded in reason they cannot be Destroyed by logic." Tyron Edwards.

On another subject, it was noted that, in the recent past, a poll was taken among blacks that asked: "With whom do you feel you have stronger ties—Africa or America? To my surprised, the majority of blacks (62%) said Africa. This leads me to question just where their loyalties are: with the nations of Africa or the United States?

Since, the great majority were born as Americans, shouldn't their allegiance be to the nation of birth? Are they saying that they would sooner live in Africa? Also, many blacks of today say they owe no loyalty to this nation! If they have no loyalty to this nation by now, my question is when will they become loyal citizens—if ever?

I believe that, by far, the majority of black Americans do hold this nation in high esteem and are loyal and patriotic citizens. Yes, there may be a few blacks that would disagree with me, but not many! For the few who would, they seem to forget, it was the nations of Africa that first enslaved your people and then sold them on the world market. Knowing this, how could they still have strong feelings for those who would do such a thing to their own kind?

Among the earliest of civilizations today, the nations of Africa are still the poorest and most under-developed Nations in the World. What is it that the blacks of today, now living in American, find so great about these nations that they have such strong feelings for?

The nations of Africa, it appears, have done little to improve the status of their people. If they have, I sure would like to know what it is! This leads me to the question, is it only skin color that matters! Think about it, how could anyone, of any race, say that they would be better off living in Africa. Why would any black have an affinity for a country that sold them into slavery? Are they saying that, after all, the color of ones skin does matter?

I cannot understand those black nations that, in this day and age, are still starving there people to such a degree that they are dying by the thousands. Why don't their Governments provide them with some form of welfare such as the blacks in America receive. Heck they don't even provide for their own citizens let alone for black citizens in other countries. Yet, the black Leadership, within this nation, continually harps on how bad we treat the blacks in America—Insisting, to this day, that the white man, because of slavery or colonization, is responsible for their present day lower status in life. A life that by any standard of measurement, is far better and more advanced then any of your fellow backs, in African, could ever hope to realize.

Today, some blacks in America still blame their failures on the white man. Africans still blame the white Europeans—their former colonial "bogyman" for their failures. When factually they, when left to their own ingenuity, did not show any signs of progressive development. It was only after colonization that the nations of Africa began to show any signs of progress. No African nation, up to that point, the Fourteenth century, had developed a calendar, written a language or domesticated an animal. Also, in this time frame, they knew how to make iron; yet they did not take advantage of this knowledge.

Far from holding the nations of Africa back, it was colonization that brought economic development to them. It was the white Europeans who built the Roads, the Railroads, the Schools. Also they provided running water, communications facilities and so on, on the African Continent. As of now, there is little evidence that left on there own initiatives, they would have accomplished little of the above. We need only to look to Haiti or even Liberia to readily see how well they, people from Africa and former slaves, when left to their own devices, would have prospered!

It could be said that some blacks over all these years, still harbored an inbred hatred for "whitey." I don't know what the answer is, but until we find out why there is such innate dislike, by some blacks, for white people or even whites for blacks, racial conflicts will continue.

Overall, however, the white man on the whole has done a lot for the blacks of Africa and continues to do so. I challenge anyone of the black race, now living in this country to, with facts, show me or any other white man, what nation of color has done as much—Just one!

As written in his book, Markets and Minorities by: Thomas Sowell, he wrote: "One of the Bases of claims for compensation reparations to contemporary blacks for the enslavements of their ancestors are that the whites in general profited, even if they were not slave owners and even If the ancestors arrived after slavery was abolished…But if the baseline…were that baseline where these descendents would be if their ancestor had never been enslaved? If that baseline is the difference between the average standard of living in Africa compared to the average standard of living of black Americans, the grotesque conclusion of this arithmetic might be that blacks pay whites compensation…"

> "May I tell you why it seems to me a good thing for us to remember wrong that has been done to us that we may forgive it." Charles Dickens.

Chapter III

White Slavery

Nearing the end of the Nineteenth Century, this nation fought a War, a Civil War to, in part, free the black slaves. Nearing the end of the Twentieth Century, we once again enslaved a class of people—the two-parent, middle class, working citizens now enslaved to the *Internal Revenue Service (IRS) to support through taxation, big government spending programs. Programs designed primarily to support other segments of our society—the so-called working poor. A program fostered for a politically motivated reason. The reason being to create not a great society, but a class of people that would, for government "Freebees" give their support and vote to a political party—a party willing to meet all their demands.*

For many years now, those that feel they were being denied their rights or just had an agenda they wanted to pursue, sold their vote to a party willing to enslave the productive part of our society to provide the money to support these "bleeding heart" initiatives/programs. As a consequence this nation, in a relatively few short years went from a depth free Society to a debtor nation. Also, our citizens have been divided into two classes of citizens—the takers and, of course, the givers. Now, more frequently referred to as the "Poor versus the Rich."

So far, this has worked to the determinant of the productive part of our citizens, the middle Class workers that has to have both parents working, just to pay the taxes necessary to support this socialistic agenda. Unless our citizens wake up, take back our country, through reasoned political actions they, the industrial and productive members of our society, by being over-taxed, will be enslaved to provide the necessities of life for the supposed underclass citizens, "From here to "Eternity."

Have you ever asked yourself how is it that the term the "Squeaky-Wheel gets the Grease" Is now such a major part of our natural dialog? It is because this nation has so many groups making noises about getting their share, that government largess has reached the point where, in effect, our liberal government is now telling the working middle class that the government can, no longer afford to give them a tax cut! Plainly, they are saying that you don't deserve to keep the money you earn. That government needs it to maintain it's socialistic agenda. Talk about A double "Whammy". First, through high taxes, you have to work extra hours, just to pay them, the taxes. Secondly, you have to deny your family in order to support other families, as selected by big government.

If you have not, as yet, come to the realization that the Middle Class is being used to pay for and foster a liberal and socialistic agenda; it is time you woke up! This agenda, to transfer wealth from one class of citizens to another through subterfuge, under the guise of "Social Justice, Is a "scam" to insure that the productive citizens are taxed through the nose, just to support governmental largess. Yes, we are being used, abused and confused by the word game. Again, we have to ask ourselves why? Today, we are as citizens, being pitted one against the other and over these past many years, we have allowed ourselves to become tax slaves, subordinating our desires in order to meet the desires of various groups.

All to many of our people have bought into the liberals "Bleeding Heart" syndrome! So much so that we have surrendered our principals of self-reliance to those of social reliance. Today, it is the oldest maxim in the world: Divide and Conquer, that is being used against us. In short, if we continue on this path we will soon become a divided nation, divided by class envy and race.

If you doubt the intention of the liberals of this society, to dominate, control and enslave our productive citizens; how is it that so many people say they do not want a tax-cut? The answer is simple, why should they, they are the ones that profit/benefit from the tax burden of others. Tell me that the productive part of our nation is not destined to labor and slave to satisfy the wants of others. Yes, there is a percentage of our citizens who need a helping hand—from time to time. They do not deserve the right to live off the labors of others in perpetuity. Once again we are being misled by such terminology as "Social Justice." My question, just what is the meaning of Social Justice?

Well according to Bailnt Vazsonyi, in his book entitled: America's 30 years War, he points out In chapter seven that "Social Justice" is a MONUMENTAL DECEPTION. The words themselves are among the most successful deception every conceived. He goes on: "Ask a variety of people to define what "Social Justice" means, specifically, and you will get different responses. All definitions of "Social Justice" boil down to any of the following:

1. Somebody should have the power to determine what you can have, or
2. Somebody should have the power to determine what you can't have, or
3. Somebody should have the power to determine what to take away from you in order to give it to others who received it without any obligation to earn it."

If the above does not sound to you much like what is happening in the good old USA, you must be living in a self-indulgent stupor. WAKE UP!

> "Give us clear vision that we may know where to stand and what to stand for—because unless we stand for something we shall fall for anything."
> Peter Marshall.

Chapter IV

The Slave Trade

Long before the discovery of America, slavery existed in Africa, West Africa and the Southern Savanna. African rulers often enslaved war prisoners and the criminals housed in their jails were sold into the slave trade—often for shipment to distant lands and places where escape was less likely.

Many were exported across the Sahara to North Africa and sold to the Portuguese who were, briefly, in the business of buying slaves in one part of Africa and selling them in another area of Africa. This practice took place even before the demand from American Plantations, across the Atlantic, came into focus. It should be noted that slavery in Africa was very different from the slavery on a plantation. A slave in Africa, immediately upon capture, was without rights and could be killed or sold as his/her capturers desired. They continued without rights until sold to an ultimate master in Africa—or else to the Europeans for transportation across the seas.

However, in Africa, slavery was not only for the sake of money or even wealth. For them the object was to increase the size of one's own group or for military power. Therefore, in many cases, women were more desirable than men. But men and women were assimilated alike, into the masters group. Another reason for slaves was to increase the groups labor force.

The slave trade, across the Atlantic, in fact, tapped an existing African slave trade-which, over the centuries had continued to send its own people into a very different kind of slavery. Over time, it diverted increasing numbers to the coast for sale to the Europeans. Yes even then the Africa slavers, of their own race, practiced a form of diversity—a diverse slave market. The organization of the trade varied greatly from one part of African to another. In some areas/regions the Europeans even built Forts where trading could take place. For example, 27 Forts were built on the Gold Cost within 220 miles of each other. African authorities even allowed the Europeans to exercise sovereignty within the forts, charging them rents for the land the forts were built on. On the other hand, other trading posts were nothing more than unfortified houses, onshore, for the storage of trade goods. These quarters also had tightly fenced yards to hold slaves awaiting shipment.

Whatever the point of trade, customary procedures already existed by the sixteenth century. Such trade normally proceeded with a payment to the local authorities, which was, in part, a gift to the authorities, thus demonstrating good will and partly a tax. The internal trade to the cost was more diverse. Some Kingdoms, (the term Kingdoms should not be equated to Kingdoms as normally understood) In the late eighteen century, such as Dhomey, the slave trade was a royal monopoly tightly controlled for the benefit of the state. Other states, such as Futa Toro on the Senegal River, sold few slaves.

Well before the discovery of the Americas, Europeans began to set up plantations on the Atlantic Islands. Later, in the sixteenth century, similar establishments such as in the Caribbean and in Brazil were established. North America, factually, was never the major procurer/user of slaves. In this regard Brazil and Argentina played a greater roll in the importation of slaves into the continents of the Americas. Also, it is well known that these countries treated their slaves badly and in fact, worked millions of them to death.

Some form of slavery or forced labor was useful for other reasons as well. The natural conditions of frontier regions with plenty of land and few people were ready for the use of slave labor. For example, as the Indian population declined in Mexico and Peru, the Spanish turned Increasingly to various forms of peonage. In Europe, the bonds of serfdom where tightened. The solutions found for the Continents of the Americas—which consisted of numerous tropical lowlands—was slavery.

Africans were not the only forced immigration to the New Word. Convicts, unsuccessful rebels against their governments and indentured workers who, more or less, bound themselves, voluntarily, to serve for a period of years, were shipped off to the Americas in large numbers, especially to Brazil. Also, Indians were enslaved and used for plantation labor. However, of the sources for slave labor in the tropics, it was apparent that Africans seemed to have special qualities in this respect and, as workers in such climates, they seemed to have superior abilities that were attributed to the Negro race, but modern knowledge of epidemiology shows that early environment as opposed to race is the true explanation.

However, in this new trading community, West Africans played, almost from the first, an indispensable part of the history of their peoples as slaves, in countries throughout the world. No one can question the violations that occurred in the world, including in the nations of Africa. In this respect the African Negro was paramount in enduring these transgressions.

However, all the transgressions were not by slave owners or plantation owners and, as fact, blacks, the sellers of their own people, were guilty of the most heinous crimes against their fellow man. These facts, when discussing the slave trade are seldom referred to in Political Correct (PC) discourse. Still it must not go unsaid or unspoken. If one is to speak factually, all the facts should be on the table. It is not, and never has been, only the white man that was guilty of such atrocities. It was equally, if not greater among the Africans. As we know, the slaves to be further sold were, in almost all cases, first enslaved by their black brothers as a result of Tribal Warfare. The claim that Slavers initiated tribal wars in order to acquired slaves, are bogus!

It should also be noted that those captured in warfare, were either enslaved in one way or another or, in many cases, they experienced despicable and merciless torture and, for many death. For those who showed exceptional courage in battle, they would have their hearts cut out and eaten in the belief that they would, in this manner, acquire the courage of the one whose heart was eaten. In many cases the captives would be cannibalized.

Yes cruelty in the slave trade was a two way street. Their "Bloods" that first captured them were in many ways, crueler to them—their captured brothers, than the white slave traders. "Condemn one you must condemn all."

All the participants displayed traits of cruelty—equally! One can truly say, in the slave trade—there were no good guys! Therefore the blame should be equally shared. Even today, in the nations of Africa, slavery in one form or another still exists. Not to mention the unspeakable and horrific suffering being imposed on them. If you want to discuss mans inhumanity to man, one only needs to look to some of the Nations of Africa. In the present day history, in many of the African Nations, slavery in one form or another still exists. Also, the truth is that the Hutu and Tutsi fractions of Africa society killed more of their people in one year, as were killed In North America during the entire period of its involvement in slavery.

Only recently, in the Southern Sudan, slavery once again returned big time in Africa, where thousands of women and children are being taken into bondage. And not to long ago, the citizens of Ethiopia, Somalia and others were being starved to death or otherwise killed by their War Lords. For example: over a million people lived in a 30,000 square mile area of the Nuba Mountain in the Sudan—as written by Brain Eads and published in the Reader's Digest—that was once home to 50 black tribes however, after ten years of war, only a few of them remain! By way of comparison, what they have done to their own, the slaves of Americas Southern Plantations were, relatively speaking, treated well.

Today, there is a lot of myth as opposed to fact, regarding slavery. For example:

Myth -   Africa was a primitive Continent.
Fact -   It was not primitive if Africa was in fact primitive, a large-scale slave trade would not have been possible.
Myth -   American, or better stated, the white race was responsible for slavery.

Fact - A developed commercial slave trade/network was already in existence in both West Africa and the Southern Savanna, long before the American Continents were even discovered; as well as long before the United States became a nation, the European countries set up plantations in the Mediterranean Islands as well as in southern Spain and Portugal. Not to mention in some of the Atlantic Islands, such as: the Canaries or Madeira. By the sixteenth century, they included Sao Thombe in the Gulf of Guinean and, as previously noted, in the Caribbean and Brazil.

Myth - Africans, during this period of the slave trade were the only ones sold into slavery or enforced immigrations and bondage.

Fact - As previously mentioned there were others, such as: Convicts, Indians and Indentured servants.

Myth - The largest number of slaves were purchased by the America Plantation owners.

Fact - They only purchased about 20%. The countries of Argentina and Brazil purchased the other 80%.

Myth - North American slave-owners were the harshest and cruelest of the owners.

Fact - North American slaves were treated in most cases to a life better than they would have had as slaves in other parts of the world—including in their homelands. In fact the great majority survived their slavery years in America, while in other nations, the great majority of them were worked to death.

Myth - The slave trade was allowed to exist because of the primitive conditions of African societies and the natural docility of these people.

Fact - Slave revolts were a common and standard feature— particularly in the Tropics of the Americas. Haiti was the first non-European country to overthrow colonial rule. Less known slave revolts were scattered throughout the backcountry of South America and the larger Caribbean Islands.

Myth - Africans were considered lazy people and only good for slave work.

Fact - They were highly valued for their ability to work hard and under hot tropical conditions.

Myth - Africa was not allowed to prosper because all its good men/women were sold off in the slave trade.

Fact - Africa was not allowed to prosper because of its tribal diversity. It is stated there were, at times, over a thousand African languages/dialects spoken. As a consequence, they could not, effectively, converse with each other. Because of this, they could not easily learn to read or write outside their tribal communities.

Myth - Africans sold into slavery were, supposedly, the cream of the crop.

Fact - In many cases, one could rightly say that they were the dregs of their society. It is factually known that many were sold into slavery to empty out the prisons. Also, many were Captives of tribal warfare and as such, many of them were sold on the slave market.

Myth - African slave traders were not aware of the hazardous and terrible conditions that the slaves would be forced to endure while being transported across the seas.

Fact - They, the Africa slave traders, knew exactly what the conditions were and even prepared the future slaves, for several months, by providing them limited food, water or exercise, to condition them for the trip.

As one can readily see, there is a lot of the truth that has been twisted and even manufactured, regarding the slave trade. We cannot, unwittingly, accept much of what is said, without first questioning it. Let it be said that slavery, as such, was a disgraceful shame on all who participated in it, from both sides—the seller, as well as the buyer! All participants must share the blame equally!

> "Not only do I pray for it, on the score of human dignity, but I can clearly foresee that nothing but the rooting out of slavery can perpetuate the

existence of our union, by consolidating it in a Common bond of principle." Attributed to George Washington.

Chapter V

The origin of slavery and slavery in America

If we were to listen to the Black Leadership and many of their followers, one would have to believe that the white man, to obtain control over the black man, originated slavery. What are the Realities?

The origin of slavery rests in the black nations of Africa and in the Middle East. This cannot be denied and students of black history can only come to this same conclusion. Today, the nations that continue to practice slavery are the same nations noted above.

Whereas, in the United States, by the Emancipation Proclamation of 1863, all slaves within the rebellious states were freed and, in 1865, by the Thirteenth Amendment to the Constitution all slaves in the United States were freed.

Today, the whites are being blamed for, supposedly, the "sins of their fathers," despite the fact that no one living today, or in the recent past, was a slave or a slave owner. Why then are we, the whites of this country only now being singled out for past deeds, of which they had no part or participation in? Could the reason be that some black lawyers can only see white, like in "Fleece?" Are we, the whites going to allow ourselves to be, like Sheep, passively skinned alive?

Will we allow others to hold us to a higher standard, just because we are born white? Will we, once again, become the "Scapegoats" for the supposed ills of others.

Some of our citizens who will never be satisfied with only equal rights—will always want more and more! Having said this, let's look at the realities:

1. Slavery began in prehistoric times and has been practiced ever since, on people of all races and in one form or another, i.e. serfdom, indentured servitude, the slave trade and so on.

2. In 3500 B.C., many were enslaved by the Sumerians of Mesopotamia (Now Iraq).
3. At this time, 3500 B.C., slavery existed in Assyria, Babylon, Egypt, Persia and other ancient societies of the Middle East. Also, slavery was practiced in ancient China as well as India.
4. Slavery was also practiced during the period of the Old Testament. From the time of Abraham, the Hebrew Patriarchs had slaves or were slaves themselves. After their escape from Egypt, the Hebrews maintained slaves among themselves, which was regulated by the Laws of Moses as a basic part of their culture and economy.
5. Slavery, as practiced in ancient times, was unknown in medieval Europe. It came into practice, in Europe, in the Fifteenth Century when slavery was introduced by the Portuguese.

It is clear that the white European, Anglo Saxons were "Johnny Come Lately" in the business of slavery. Also, that Africans were at the forefront of slavery and in the slave trade across the Atlantic. One could say that the Nations of Africa were the "WAL-MARTS" of the slave trade. Students of black history should have learned the truth of their races participation in the selling of their people into slavery. The truth being that it was the nations of Africa that were the exporters of slaves on a global basis. Also, in some African nations, slavery exists to this day, in one form or another.

The slave trade to the settlements in the new world, America, was Introduce into the colonies In 1619 when several Africans were landed and sold into slavery by a Dutch slave trader, in Jamestown, Virginia. In 1715 there were about twenty-three thousand slaves in Virginia and approximately the same number in Maryland and the Carolinas.

By the beginning of the Nineteenth Century, there were about 1,500.000 slaves in America. In the year 1860, just prior to the Civil War, the slave states had about four million slaves or about a third of the South's population. To place slavery in perspective, the total population of America, At this time was about 30,000.000 and was an almost equally divided population between the North and Southern parts of this nation, which consisted, in total, of 26 states. It should be noted, that at this time, there were about 500,000 blacks in the Northern part of the states that were called "Freemen." Some of them also participated in slavery and had slaves.

As one can readily see, even during the peak period of slavery in America, the vast majority of people never owned a slave, even in the South. One could ask, with a total population today, of 284,000.000 people, of which the majority is white, why are all whites in this day and age being blamed for the acts of a few, relatively speaking, of our citizens that were slaveholders.

Reparations would not be an act for justice, but for profit, to be derived from a particular race of people—the white race! How else can they determine who is to pay and who is not! So—what it their solution—make them all pay! To justify this line of reasoning, they are taking it upon themselves to say that all white men now and in the past, benefited from slavery. This cannot be supported by fact.

If the blacks of today can look to the past and find blame in the white man, can't they also see fault in their own race. A race of people who enslaved millions of their own and for what—financial gain! Folks slavery was a two-way street and it is on the shores/coast of Africa, that the "Slave Coast" is located. Slavery was a two-way trading relationship, however for slaves it was a one-way street out of Africa. It is the African Nations that must take the blunt of the blame for the enslavement of their ancestors. Africa provided the slaves. Without slaves, there could have been no slave trade and thus no black slavery.

Today, as a nation, we have people of all races, creeds and colors. Still, in our country, it seems that only the white man is singled out as the perpetrator of all the ills of the other races. Yes, in America we have finally broken the color barrier. When it comes to looking for someone to blame, some of the other races can only see WHITE.

However, history shows that the white race has done more to rid itself of slavery, particularly in the United States of America, than any other race of people on the face of this planet. No other nation can make this statement. To support this premise, the following facts are enumerated:

1. During the l700's, many persons of the time, as well as religious leaders in Europe And North America came to condemn slavery. Particularly black slavery!
2. Many more Americans turned against slavery during the Revolutionary period: l773-1783. The State of Vermont in l777 was the first state to abolish slavery, followed by Massachusetts in l783. Pennsylvania called for the gradual abolition of slaver in 1780, Rhode Island in 1784 and New York in l799. The importation of slaves into the United States. After the year 1808, was forbidden by an act of congress.
3. During the year's l837-1860, a strong abolitionist movement existed in many parts of the United States of America.

Not only was slavery in the United States being rejected, by many, it was also experiencing rejection in several European countries. France in l754 was the first nation to abolish slavery. Slavery in the French colonies, however, was re-established in 1802 and finally ended in l848. Haiti in l804 was the first nation to abolish slavery in the Western hemisphere. This was followed by Spain's colonies during the period 1808-1825. England abolished slavery in l772 and the English colonies in l833. Spain ended slavery in Puerto Rico in 1873. Slavery, in Cuba was ended in l886 and Brazil in l888. History has shown that although the white races of the world did take up slavery; they were also the first to take steps to end slavery. No nation or nations, throughout the world, can match the United States of America, as having paid the highest price of all, because of the Civil War, to rid itself from slavery.

Still, there are amongst us, those that would have us pay for things that happened in our past not of our making. To them, the fact that none of us had anything to do with slavery is of little or no consequence.

Slavery, by definition, is a practice in which people own other people. A slave is the property of his or her owner, works without pay, but is compensated by food, shelter and clothing. The great tragedy of slavery is the loss of "freedom by the slave." In North America slavery, in the South, flourished. The north, however was not so dependant on slave labor because of differing economic needs/requirements. During the years 1600-1700's most slaves worked on plantation in the South that grew indigo, rice and cotton. With the invention of the cotton gin by Eli Whitney, in 1793, large-scale production of cotton began. As a result, more slaves were required. The high demand for cotton led to the establishment and growth of many additional cotton plantations.

In the 1800's the majority of plantation slaves worked in the fields planting and/or picking cotton. House slaves, as they were called, had a more typical master-servant relationship. They lived in their masters/owner's home, worked few hours and had more privileges. The hard/bad part of this was that they were always subject to the call or bidding of the master. The majority of slaves that, over-time, were freed by their owner's were house slaves.

Many plantation slaves became skilled workers such as, blacksmiths, carpenters, bricklayers, etc., many others became construction workers. They also worked as Dockworkers, Lumberjacks, Office workers and Riverboat pilots. Still others worked in factories and in the Mines. Also, on the plantations, some were housed as well as freemen but many more field hands lived under the worst of conditions.

To entice and or encourage their slaves to willing obedience, some slave owners treated there slaves kindly: while others relied on punishment such as lashings, denial of adequate food, etc., to force them to work harder. In the South, state laws prohibited the education of slaves. Because of necessity, however, the slaves developed their own language.

Religion, a mixture of African and Christian beliefs, played a role in their lives. Many slaves tried to escape to freedom and thousands succeeded in doing so. Many of these escapes were accomplished via the "underground railroads." Slavery played a major roll in the economic development of the nation and cotton picked by the slaves, became the nations most valuable export, during this period of time In our history.

In contrasting the life of a Negro slave, with that of a white "wage-slave" during the I800's; it was claimed in 1854, by Irish workers, that the only difference between a Negro slave of the South and white "wage-slaves" of the North is that one had a master without asking for it and the other had to beg for the privilege of becoming a slave. On the face of it, this has some merit. The white man, many of Irish descent, had to work many hours a day for a mere pittance of fifty cents per-day. Out of his earnings, he had to provide for all the necessities of life, such as, food, clothing, housing and medical needs. Plus whatever else he might need for his meager existence. At the end of his working years he had no retirement income and was, in effect turned adrift and, in many cases, forced to beg for the rest of their lives.

In contrast, the slave owners of the South, fed and clothed their slaves, provided shelter, medical care and the many other necessities that were required. Also, at the end of their lives, they were properly buried. Given the two ways of life, was it not the white male of the time who also was enslaved to his labors? Sure they had some freedom of sorts but with little money, they were also limited in their choices as well as liberties.

The slave in the United States, when considering the realities, were treated better then they would have been, had they remained slaves in their various homelands. History will bear this out!

Also, as we know how they were treated in Africa, one might conclude that some blacks lives were possible saved by being enslaved in America. Surly no one can deny that their descendants did fair much better. As a group, the blacks of America are among the riches blacks in the world. Formed as a nation, they would be the fifth richest country in the world.

After the Civil War, in the period known as Reconstruction, the Union was restored and the rebuilding of the south began. Reconstruction however did not solve the problems of the South or the problems of the blacks. Few blacks acquired land and the independence they thought, as freedmen, they would have. Instead most of them continued to work for the former master, doing the same labor they had performed as slaves. Some worked for low pay, others became sharecroppers. Of the 4,000.000 blacks in the South, after the Civil War, many of them migrated to the North. However, many of them returned to the South, of their own volition.

> "The only freedom which deserves the name is that of pursuing our own good in our own way, So long as we do not attempt to deprive others of theirs, or impede their efforts to obtain it." John Stuar.

Chapter VI

Black Racism

What is hardly ever noticed or given due attention are blacks segregating themselves from our society as a matter of choice. They do not consider themselves Americans. By choice, they have elected to be called African-Americans. I ask, if an America went to African and became a citizen would he than become an American-African?

In his book America's 30 Years War, Balint Vazonyi states the following:

> "...Being "African" in America amounts to an artificial nationality. There really is no such thing as an "African-American." People so designated are "Americans-whose-distant-ancestry-is-somewhere-on-the-African-continent."

In short if you were born in America, you are American. It seems to me that those who, not to long ago, cried out for an end to racial segregation, have elected to separate themselves by how they choose to be called, i.e., Black Panthers, The Negro College Fund and The (black) Nation of Islam etc. For years they claimed that the color of their skin should not matter. However, to them, it does matter—a lot! Is it that blacks don't mind being separated by color?

Not long ago it was stated, in essence, that blacks couldn't be racist because there are more whites than blacks. Well we know better, don't we? There is black racism against the whites, but more than that, there is also racism against blacks by blacks. If the truth were known, In today's world, some blacks are just as racist as some whites, if not more so. If you doubt this, I suggest you talk to people of the Asian races—particularly the Koreans. Have you noticed that when they riot in the streets, almost at the drop of a hat, it is usually the Asian stores that get hit the hardest. Many white owners of small stores, long ago learned not to locate in the black Districts.

Never mind the other races blacks have, for political purposes and over all these many years, turned on their people. Why, because these people—these black people—are not willing to say that they are inferior, that they can't make it on their own, that they need special privileges and so forth. Because of their stand, they are labeled as "Uncles Tom's."

In spite of this, many blacks will not be mis-lead. They do not consider them selves to be Incompetents. They know that they are just as capable as any other man or women, regardless of race. They know that they are fully capable of making it on their own—without imposed Government assistance.

Still, all too many have accepted this nonsense—that they can't make it on their own—as fact. They need only look around to see the many people of their race that have and will continue to make it on their own! They did not accept the words of their supposed leaders that they needed Affirmative action—they took firm action and responsibility for their lives. They did not accept or limit themselves to government quotas but established their own personal goals.

The blacks are a great race of people—they are survivors— and I don't mean survivors of slavery. Many of their race are survivors because they have shown that they can take the hard knocks and roll with the punches as good or better than most. Unfortunately, there are still many within the black race that willingly let themselves be called a "lesser person" by their leaders. It is by their supposed leaders that they are being hailed as inferior beings. Why? Simply stated, If you can make it on your own, you don't need them!

For this reason, you are also being led to believe that all "Cops" are out to get the black man. Not true! If the truth is known, blacks kill more blacks, across this nation, in one year, than have ever been killed by law enforcement officials, in our nations entire history!

Recently, Charleton Heston, in his speech at the Harvard Law Forum said: "...A few years Back I heard about a rapper named Ice-T who was selling a CD called "Cop Killer" celebrating ambushing and murdering police officers..." I would like to ask you, if you were a "Cop" would you not feel a little insecure on the job, knowing that there are people just looking for a reason to kill you. Those songs/words are being spread, by virtue of supposed entertainment, encouraging others—to kills COPS! Wouldn't you, if you were a cop, feel a little insecure on the job and perhaps a little quick to respond?

It is easy to turn your hatred on others. This is well known amongst us, that there are "Cop Haters," regardless of their color. If you can hate all cops, you therefore hate cops of your race, as there are many in this field. As such, it is black racism against fellow blacks.

Mr. Heston went on reading more of the words from Cop killers, every vicious vulgar, Instructional one:

> I got my 12 gauge sawed off.
> I got my headlights turned on off.
> I'm about to bust some shots off.
> I'm about to dust some cops off...

Now I ask you, as a Police Officer, on the job, do you feel that these words might give one pause about feeling secure. Do you not think that, just maybe, if you were in this situation, that you might also feel a little nervous and yes, even scarred when a black confronts you while in the commission of a crime. How would you, in such a confrontation react, knowing you only have 1/16 of a second to decide to shoot or not to shoot! In whose favor would you decide?

As we know, Jesse Jackson as well as Al Sharpton are quick to charge the police with making many rash decisions. Yes, they are quick to judge others, particularly our men in blue. Do they do this in a rational way? NO! It is done in a manner to insure they bring out the worst in all to many of us. However, many still feel that without the cops to hate, they would have to accept blame for their faults and or failures. For a change, instead of being quick to condemn others, they should first try walking in the shoes of those they are quick to blame.

Ask yourself, why are so many people, of different races, now numbering over 170 nationalities, that have come to this country; the downtrodden citizens of other countries—countries that they are willing to forsake—giving up everything they have, to come to the good old USA, looking for a chance to make it own their own. I wonder how many who came here, by whatever means, would willingly give it all up and go back to whence they came. I think they would be few in number, if any! Being in this great land of ours, they have come to know that if you can't make it here in America, you probably can't make it anywhere. This is the land of opportunity for those willing to work at it. No successful person has made it on the Welfare line!

Recently I heard a black man talking on a TV program to another black man who was filled with hatred for people of the other races. This man, in response to the others complaints said, in effect, "I don't wake up each morning, look in the mirror and see 'Victim' written across my forehead." In these few words, he said it all. He is a man—a self made man! HE WILL NEVER BE A SLAVE TO ANY MAN OR POLITICAL PARTY. He will always be his own man. For him and those of his ilk, they deserve the highest respect. And yes, there are many just like him in the black race! How do I know this? Because, over my many years, I have come to know a lot of them! They know that one does not have to lower oneself to make it in this world, that they can stand proud and walk tall among their fellow man!

Still, among all to many blacks, we are finding those in our midst that want to destroy the white man's heritage by attacking our founding fathers, our nations flag and yes, the Confederate flag. These people who seek only to divide the races for, I guess, personal satisfaction or political gain are, only now it seems, coming out of the woods. Finally, they are admitting that they feel no loyalty to this country and, in fact, will admit that will not say the "Pledge of Allegiance" to our flag. Yes they will accept the fruits of this country, but feel no gratitude for it. By comparison with the Nations of Africa, the bountiful life this land has provided them means nothing. They have no sense of gratitude let alone loyalty; never looking at or realizing what they have gained as a result of their ancestor's enslavement.

For Example, there is still a loud and endless cry by many blacks for "Affirmative" action, giving blacks preferential treatment when enrolling for college. I do not understand this demand. Prior to World War II few of our nations children—white or black—went to college. The reason was not because of race. It was because they could not afford it. Should we now go back to that generation and give preference to their decedents, regardless of race, when they try to get Into college? Also, when did going to college become an entitlement—for any race!

> "Perfect freedom is reserved for the man who lives by his own work and in that work does what he wants to do." Robin George Colligwood.

Chapter VII

Equal Rights—Civil Disorder

Berry Goldwater, in his nomination speech at the Republican Parties convention Stated, in part: "...this party, with its every action, every word, every breath and every heartbeat has but a single resolve and this is: "Freedom."

Freedom made orderly for this nation by our constitutional government. Freedom balanced so that order, lacking liberty, will not become the slavery of the prison cell, balanced so that liberty, lacking order, will not become the license of the mob of the Jungle..."

Goldwater's address was given in 1964. Today, it should be noted, once again, that the rights of all people of this nation are equal and this must be maintained. These rights must be maintained by lawful branches of our government and the legitimate authorities.

However, it appears that a class of people are given "Special Rights." That, if for some reason they disagree with a law, a police action, a court decision, they have the right to take to the streets in violent protest. In short, they seem to feel that if they don't get their way; they have a right to riot. This was only recently demonstrated in the City of Cincinnati, Ohio.

They, the blacks in Cincinnati, may have had a legitimate compliant, they did not have the right to riot in the streets. We are a nation of Laws, not of mob rule. For to long now, this nation, under the guise of civil equity have given the blacks of this nation, a belief that they are above the law. Tell me what other race of people; out of the 170 various nationalities of our citizens have, at a whim, decided to take to the streets, just because they think they are not getting the justice that they feel is owed to them. Why? Because of their ancestors slavery. Well, for their information, every race of people, in some manner or another have suffered under various forms of slavery and or depredation. They, the blacks, are not exclusive to this form of humiliation. It is time that they realize this fact of life. Not getting ones way—does not give one permission to take the law into their hands. NO ONE IS [OR SHOULD BE] ABOVE THE LAW!

What has recently occurred in Cincinnati is not the first instance of this nature. Major riots have, over the years and across this nation, for some blacks, become a way of life for many blacks. It is hard to find that so many riots over the years, are the result of community concern or care for their fellow man. If they are, why do we have so much destruction of others property? Why do they attack innocent people, drag them from their cars just to beat on them? How is it that they do these things when they are, supposedly, seeking justice? Are these the acts of concerned citizens? I don't think so! For the most part, they are simply opportunists, looking for a chance to steal and destroy. They are following the Laws of the Jungle—the hell with the laws of the land.

What has been their punishment when caught in these acts? For the most part, they are left off the "hook" with little if any punishment! After all, they are descendants of slaves. Today we are learning that we are not only our brother's keepers, we are also the keepers of many of our black citizens. Because they have lived, supposedly, a hard life, we must let them roam free to wantonly steal and destroy with impunity and without fear of the law.

For example, even those that end up in prison for breaking the law, while incarcerated, they get:

1. Free housing—with free heating, air conditioning, bathroom facilities, electricity, cable TV and, in fact, all the amenities found in a first rate motel.
2. Free health care, religious counseling, legal counseling, entertainment, Playboy magazines, transportation, clothing, recreational equipment and meals.

And to top it all off—free conjugal visits. Oh my, how cruel can we, as a nation, get!

Guess what, some blacks are now complaining that they, the prisoners/convicts, don't have the right to vote. Shucks, all they did was break the law. Why do we need a Welfare State? Hell, just break the law, go to prison and "ZHAZAM" welcome to Utopia.

Like fools, the taxpayers will provide them with all the freebees they could possibly want—all they have to do is get imprisoned. Could this explain why so many blacks are in prison? As l2% of our nations population, they account for 47% or our nations Prisoners.

In today's world, you do not need to have ambition, a willingness to work, or a sense of personal responsibility. In fact, if you want to live a good life, have no personal inhibitions, no personal or moral values—just become a criminal and, in short order, you will hear those special words, "welcome to prison." Yes a federal prison that will provide all the aforementioned goodies plus tennis courts, swimming pools, weekend passes and oh "hell," what more does one need!

It was once said: "the greatest danger to a civilized nation is the man who has no stake in it and nothing to lose by rejecting all that civilization stands for." Henry Ford II. Every race of people, at times, has had to face hardships and adversity, in one form or another. The black leadership of this country has been crying out so much, that you would think the blacks of this nation are the only ones that had to "overcome."

It is their leadership, the black leaders of this nation who, for the most part, are willing to tell the blacks that, as a race; you are incompetent, incapable and unable to make it on your own. Unfortunately, all to many blacks have played into their hands. Not only that, you have also been taken in by the white "bleeding hearts" of this nation, who willingly put you down as incompetents, just so they can "feel good" by, supposedly helping you. Helping you to remain, so to speak, helpless. As such, you become more dependant on them for your salvation. In short, like it or not, they are little by little, enslaving you to their political agenda. So far they, the bleeding hearts, are winning! All To many of you have been willing to sell you soul to the company store.

Why have so many of you accepted, without reservation, that you need: set-asides, quotas, affirmative action and such? Why have you allowed your leadership to put you down? As a strong and proud people—I do not understand how you can, willingly, be so degraded and for what—government pork! You must know, it was the slave owners who used this method to entice your ancestors to work harder? Now you're political leadership is using it to enslave you to them. For what—a pound of flesh!

I ask, what is equal about being treated as incompetents. Why are you, as a black person, so willing to admit that you are unable to get along in the world—without the help of big daddy government. Frankly, I can't understand why so many blacks are willing to accept this put down of your race. Why are you so ready and willing to accept being relegated as a lesser human being. If the truth is that we are all born equal; how is it that your leadership can say your not?

Also, you are being used by words, words that are designed to make you mad and incite you to act without reason. If you are convinced, that you are being PROFILED, I have some questions regarding this complaint:

1. Are only blacks being profiled?
2. Is it black profiling if a black mans picture is on a wanted poster?
3. If, on the evening TV news, a security camera within the store shows that it is a black man robbing the store, is it profiling?
4. If a black man robs me and I give a description of him as the perpetrator in regards to his skin color, hair and such, am I profiling him only because he is black.
5. If a black person attempts to force me into giving him money or personal property, by saying he will see that my business is boycotted. If I reported the attempted extortion, describing the person who made the treat, would I be Profiling?

In view of the aforementioned, could I as a white man:

6. Do the same as Jesse Jackson or Al Sharpton, and go across the nation as a self-appointed arbiter of the law and how it should apply when the matter concerns a white person?
7. Could I form a group of white citizens, make false charges against the blacks for denying me my civil rights or is this right exclusive to blacks?
8. Could I, as a white man, go to some public event, such as a parade and feel free to abuse women in a sexual manner as some citizens of color recently did?
9. Can I, as a white man, also disagree with a juries decision and feel free to start a riot?
10. Can a white man play the "race card" or is this an exclusive right of a black person?
11. Can a white man clap laugh and jump for joy when a white person is acquitted of killing a black man.

As a Nation, we have all paid a high price for the slavery of the past. However, it was the slaves, the ones actually enslaved, that paid the highest price of all. Slavery, without a doubt, was a tragic event, first started in the nations of Africa and North Africa and eventually crossed the oceans. However, the past is the past. Crying about it or holding it against those that had nothing to do with it—does not help! You cannot hold others responsible for that of which they had nothing to do with.

Making such claims, as Reparations, will not serve anyone and, in fact, would be a disservice to both races—for it would only divide us. You cannot blame the white man of today, for the acts of his ancestors. As most blacks of this great nation, you also have ancestors of the slave trade to thank for your present day privilege of living in this country. Today, the blacks of this nation have advanced beyond any expectations of their ancestors—the ones who paid the price—for your present prosperity. No place in the world, including Africa, could the decedents of slaves, have obtained such prosperity.

You, the present day blacks of this nation, are the beneficiaries of their benefactors, the ones who suffered the slavery—should you now attempt to belittle there sacrifice— only to enrich yourselves. Instead, you should count your blessings. Your ancestors lost their freedom, labored and died—never knowing or experiencing the life you now find yourself living in. Reparations paid to you who are reaping the benefits of their misfortune would be like "spitting on their graves." They deserve better. It would be an affront to your race, to take some advantage from their enslavement over and above what you have already gained.

> "A sound body is a first-class thing, a sound mind is an even better thing, but the thing that counts for most in the individual as in the nation, is character, the sum of those qualities which make man a good man and a women a good women."
> Theodore Roosevelt.

Chapter VIII

Black vs. Blue—Plus Free Speech

Our nation is, within the framework of color, being further divided. However, instead of black on white, we are embodied in a black on blue confrontation, of which the latest was in the City of Cincinnati, Ohio.

Such confrontations are not new to our relatively recent national history. In his book, "The making of the President," published in 1964, Theodore H. White, in matters to come, regarding race, he was, extremely profound, if not prophetical, concerning future occurrences. In his book he calls to our attention, as we can recall, Black versus Blue confrontations, resulting in the blacks rioting in the streets.

This situation occurred between an apartment superintendent and a black youth by the name of James Powell whereby, in an escalating situation, Powell was threatening that he was going to cut that "blankty, blankty, superintendent" As he was walking across the street, to act on his threat, by chance, an off duty policeman had come on the scene and challenged Powell, ordering him to drop the knife. To enforce his order, the officer fired a warning shot causing Powell to lunge, slashing and cutting the officers right forearm. In response, the police officer fired twice, killing his attacker. Seventy-two hours later, the New York City riot of 1964 erupted.

In his book, Mr. White makes a fortuitous statement: "The shooting of James Powell is a classic example of how, in an unstable situation, dogma and accident can escalate into explosion." The book goes on, pointing out that during this period, while the city of New York was doing the most to quell Negro problems; it was the first to experience, as Its reward, black "riots in the streets."

This situation evidently rose to a point wherein a most courageous Negro leader of that period, Roy Wilkins, executive secretary of the NAACP, in an eloquent outburst of dismay wrote: "These teen-age Negro hoodlums in New York City are undercutting and wrecking the gains made by the hundreds of Negroes and white youngsters who went to Jail for human rights.

These punks—these hot shots, tearing up sub-way cars and attacking innocent people, are selling the Freedom Riders down the river...These Harlem and Brooklyn morons...are cutting and slashing at the race's self-respect, something they can never rebuild with their knives, their baseball bats, their brass knuckles and their filthy language." Note: it is important to stress, for the record, that in that time, 1964, how splendid was the police work in New York during this week of violence, for it was almost completely ignored...

The above was true than, as it appears to be today—that is that in situations of this nature—the police are first to become suspect in violating their principals as opposed to, just maybe, they were acting within the law and doing their jobs. Today, all over this nation, our Police Officers are being derided, defamed and downgraded without getting even a nod of possible concession, that perhaps their Actions, considering the situation, were justified.

Years ago, Roy Wilkins had the guts to speak out against these marauding punks-hoods! Still many black youths of today, are creating civil disorders that only serve as an excuse to destroy and steal others property and, of course, to attack and beat-up whites—whites that had nothing to do with the situation at hand. Where is their black leaders of today? Well for the most part, on the side of the hoodlums, giving them their support, instead of dealing appropriately with these incorrigibles.

In his book, "Hating Whitey" David Horowitz, one of the few white men, of today, that will speak out on matters of black hatred for the white man, is being discriminated against, not only by the media, but also on the campuses of our nations bastions of liberalism at its worst—these institutions of non-learning now dominating our Political Correct (PC) society.

These liberal lip proponents of our constitutionality would not even give him, Mr. Horowitz, his right to speak out on many of these campuses, regarding his views on Reparations. Talk about liberal cowards. Yes, black as well as whites were, in these incidents or confrontations, just plain cowards. No question about it. Not one of them had the guts or knowledge to debate him, regarding this subject, on its merits. These screaming "mental midgets," that lacked the capacity to openly debate Mr. Horowitz are, just a bunch of "snooty-nosed" brainless idiots, lacking knowledge or personal courage. Seeing them on TV, I noticed that quite a few of the protesters obviously needed affirmative action to even go to a liberal college!

Mr. Horowitz, for those that may not be aware of it, is of Jewish ancestry and was once a strong advocate for Civil Rights and Liberalism. Now, because he got his senses back, disavowing a part of his former beliefs, he is being castigated and vilified almost beyond belief. Not only by his present day detractors but, as well, by his former, supposedly friends. So far, he has withstood the challenge—he has not let the "Cowards" Grind him down."

At times, I wonder about my fellow citizens; those that allow themselves to be dragged down to the lower levels of decency, now pervasive within a great part of our society. Yes, I know, free speech is everything; still I feel there are those that would use free speech only as it leads to their advantage or they can use it in a manner to obstruct the rights of others such as in Political Correct speech.

I hope that the aforementioned students would not be considered, even amongst the liberals, our nations best and brightest. It was obvious that that these little people, of little knowledge, did not have the courage to go one-on-one with an educated and informed person. Unfortunately, once again, the mob mentality held sway.

Today we are seeing it, more and more frequently, the mob mentality at work; not only in our streets, but also on the campuses of our supposed institutions of learning. How have we, as a nation of people willing to stand up for our rights, allowed a relatively speaking, small band of our citizens to feel free to react violently just because they are not pleased by the outcome, such as a verdict, not of their liking. How long are we, a proud law abiding people going to tolerate such unwarranted and destructive disregard for the laws of this land. No grievance, of any sort, can justify the breaking of our laws. We all have civil rights; lets use our rights in a civilized manner. Rioting in the streets helps no one, solves no problem and is not conducive to the maintenance of an orderly and civilized society.

> "We can maintain a free society only if we recognize that in a free society no one can win all the time. No one can have his own way all the time, and no one is right all the Time." Richard M. Nixon.

Chapter IX

Race—the Race Card and Majority Rule

By the year 2050, there will be no majority race in America. Will that be good for the Nation or will it only lead to more racially motivated disunity. At that time, or even earlier, the racial composition of this nation will be: Mexican/Hispanic 25%, Blacks 13%, Asians, American Indians, Pacific Islands and other none-whites 14%: for a total Population of non-whites of 52%. At that time, the white population will be 48%. As a result, we will become a minority race within our own country.

At this time the white race, the founders and builders of this great nation will lose control of their nation to a conglomeration of minorities. I know of no other nation, through out history, wherein its majority of people have or will have become a minority within their nation, by virtue of its willingness to do so. Under the overt banner of Liberalism and the covert "I feel your pain" socialism, a great many of our race, the white Race, have become complicit in this all too soon to be, loss of our nation. Yes, we will have lost our national dominance without a shoot being fired!

If a white man dares speak up on this subject, not only will the minorities berate him but all too many whites, as well. The hell with personal honor! The individual can no longer speak up for their beliefs or race. Should one do so, they will be called Racists.

We the whites have allowed ourselves to be outwitted not by deeds or actions, but by a word—that word being "RACIST." How did this come about? It came about by many of our citizens being willing to follow the Liberal line. We have allowed ourselves to fear words, such as racist. Why, because we, by doing so are not fair-minded or even just after all they have suffered so long under white dominance. I wonder since they, the blacks, will still be a minority of the minorities in the year 2050. Do they think they will be treated better by the other minorities?

Today, as a supposedly law-abiding Christian nation, we are about to go over the edge. We are no longer allowed to speak out against those of other races, because we might hurt their feelings. My question—What about our feelings? Yes, we as a people, a once proud people, have subordinated our values and, in some case our rights to the "Race Card" a card that is often played against us—the white race. To those amongst us that have nothing but ill will for us; we have forsaken our own values and self-worth. Why, to avoid being called a racist?

In the past forty years or so, our national morality, educational accomplishments, Justice system, and so-forth, has been degraded to the point destruction of our countries Moral fabric. Yes destruction to everything we, as a people as a nation, once stood for. Example:

1. We went from a debt free nation to a debtor nation, in great part, because of the "Great Society Boondoggle."
2. Our educational system, once the greatest in the world is now a "basket case" of inefficiency and inadequacy.
3. Out national medical system, in the year l960 cost this nation 26 Billion annually; now costs a trillion dollars plus, per year.
4. Our military, until recently, was being greatly eroded/dismantled.
5. Crime in the streets became a national disgrace. Only recently and in board daylight, many women were sexually fondled and otherwise harassed. While watching a parade. Persons calling themselves "Wilders" caused such acts.

Wild hell—they were acting like savages!

6. We have witnessed almost daily; verbal attacks on our free enterprise system and the continual condemnation of our successful citizens—the rich.

Even in this day and age, there are amongst us those that have no idea as to what our Country stands for, now or in the past. For example:

1. They do not have a clue as to how our nation came to be—they don't even know that it was founded by a group of people, all white, who made a Declaration of Independence pledging to each other: "Our lives, Our Fortunes and Our Sacred honor." Yes, our founding fathers were willing to forgo their all, to establish our nation. Today we lack the courage to stand up for ourselves, let alone our country.
2. Thanks to our educational system, many of our College Students cannot tell us why the Revolutionary war was fought. Also they still do not understand what the Civil War was all about.
3. For many, World War II was just a blot in our nations history.

Unless we, as a nation join together, in unity, to preserve, protect and defend our Country and all that we believe in and love—history will condemn us for our in-action in our nations time of need! We can no longer passively accept what is going on in our Nation If we do we will, by our failure to act, forever relegate our race, our people, to The "Dung Heap" of History.

One could ask, whatever happened to "Majority Rule?" How has being in the Minority, come to mean that they have priority, over the majority? In fact, this rule—Majority rule—is, supposedly how we conduct ourselves in our jurisprudence, in our Elections and in fact just about any pro-forma action, where decisions are to be made—the Majority Rules. How is it that, in recent history, all to often, the minority rules. For example: This nation is a Christian Nation and yet, the great majority of its people, about 95% have to avoid some of their religious symbolism in order not to offend someone in a minority religions. Is Christianity given this same consideration in nations where the Majority religion is, Islamic, Hinduism or of any other major religion other than Christianity? The answer to this question is a resounding "No."

In the most free of the free nations, the United States of America, it appears our majority of citizens, who are also in the majority religion—Christianity—are denied the right to worship as they would; to appease some in the minority religions by not, so to speak—hurting their feelings!

Have' we as a majority, somehow, allowed the minority to gain power through the Political Correct (PC) crowd? No, we can't hurt the feelings of others; we must subject our rights, our freedoms, our liberties to the rights of those in the minority after all we can't be mean to them. How we feel no longer matters! This is just plain nonsense. For some reason, we have succumbed to it and forfeited our civil rights, in order that we don't make others mad—at least that is what our liberal PC crowd would have us believe.

Unfortunately, all to many "bleeding hearts" of this nation, have fallen for this Political correct foolishness! UNLES WE DEMAND, ONCE AGAIN, OUR RELIGIOUS RIGHTS TO BELIEVE AND WORSHIP, AS WE SEE FIT, WE WILL SOON FIND OURSELVES LIVING IN AN ATHIEST AMERICA, IF NOT ATHIEST—BEING DOMINATED BY ALL SORTS OF MINOR RELIGIONS.

As a Nation Founded in Christianity, we must do whatever it takes to return our nation to its former Greatness, accomplished through Christian doctrine and the innate goodness and character of the MAORITY OF ITS CITIZENS!

> "Whoever seeks to set one race against another seeks to enslave all races. Whoever seeks to set one religion against another seeks to destroy all religion." Franklin D. Roosevelt.

Chapter X

Efforts to subvert the Election Process

It seems that the will of the people, as demonstrated in Florida, was almost overcome by the vain attempt of a few of our unsavory citizens, and the greedy who tried their best to subvert the election process of this great nation. Seldom, in our nations history, has a group of citizens acted in such a damaging and destructive way. Why? Because, just as in the riots, they didn't get their way!

Also, many illiterate and feeble-minded citizens were allowed to vote. This, just so Jesse Jackson could proudly proclaim to his fellow Democrats how much he was responsible for the increase in voter registration and participation. And indeed he was responsible for the increase. However, as one of his black sisters said to Jesse, "The next time you drop a car load off, make sure they know what their doing." As I understand it, a large percentage of the people in the contested voter precincts were illiterate. It wasn't just the voting machines out of whack; it was also the result of many "wacky" voters. And yes, they proudly proclaimed that every vote should be counted not only once, twice, three times and on and on, until they got the numbers they were looking for. Under the auspicious of the Democratic Party, to elect their man, come hell or high water, they were determined to let no pimple or dimple go unaccounted for—why should they, they were already willing to count the votes of the simple.

It seems to me that the nation was once again aloud to witness how the "Blame Game" is played. Blame the Machines, blame the Police, blame the Secretary of the State, blame the Governor, and blame the Supreme Court. That's right; blame everyone but the culprits. The Democrats, got the blame game down pat, however, they have no personal Shame.

In the last Presidential Election, held in the year 2000, this nations voter rights, across the nation, were subjugated to the

47

mercy of a small group of our citizens who, through Voter ignorance, senility or for one reason or another, did not even know how to vote. That's right, once they got into the voting booth, they were unable to follow even the most simple of instructions. Not only did they not know how to do it, they didn't even understand why they were doing it!

To abide by the wishes of these people, we had to bring in all kinds of lawyers, Judges, voting machine experts and even "Pimples and Dimples" into the game. Chad was no longer an African Nation, it was another spot/dot to be counted over and Over and OVER!

To satisfy a minority group, once again, who could only repeat over and over what their party leaders had thought them to say: "Every Vote Counts" they proved they could follow instructions—had they been repeatedly instructed as to how to vote and whom to vote for—perhaps they would not have been so confused. By demonstrating the ability to follow instructions, the proved they could learn, even if it had to be drummed into their heads.

If, in the future, it is only these small groups of people, in perspective—a handful of incompetents—that would hold sway over our elections process; what does it say for equal rights? Anyone of us who voted, could just as easily make false or stupid claims that would, in effect, serve to overthrow the election results. Why is it that only certain/particular groups get all the attention?

Only after the results did not favor their party's candidate, did they want to change the voting process. To accommodate their desires, like rats scampering around on the deck of a sinking ship, the will of the majority was subordinated to the will of the minority.

That's right, to appease those that are quick to cry out, "its not fair" we, THE PEOPLE as usual, gave in to their whimpering voices and lowered our standards to accommodate the minority. My question, what is fair about that? Have we become so damn diverse that only certain groups get the "grease" needed to satisfy their every demand. It is no longer equality that they are crying out for, it is the need to satisfy their little ole hearts desires—all of them. Fairness is no longer the test! Is the majority, as frequently happens in today's world, going to always be the ones that must surrender their values to satisfy the needs of minority groups. The question, in regards to fairness, is fairness to whom? What happened to just plain and simple EQUALITY?

Racial bias against the White Race is on the increase in our nation. W.B. Du Bois a deceased white man was recently being proclaimed as a "Civil Rights" giant and he was, in reality, the founder of the NAACP? He was also a strong believer in government control of the people. His loyalty to this country is questionable and could be stated as nil. Du Bois, after fully embracing communism, moved to Ghana to live out the rest of his life.

Because of Du Bois one could, factually say, that the roots of the NAACP were grounded in socialism if not outright communism. Initially, this group was supposedly a "Civil Rights" organization but, over the years, its character, as well as its dependency has become a political vessel for Liberalism as well as for blacks. One again Socialism, if not outright Communism has become entwined in the NAACP agenda.

In the last election of 2000, for the Presidency, despite G.W. Bush holding his hand out to them, for their support, a great majority of the black voters not only soundly reject him but, one could say, they "Spit in his Hand." Talk about hypocrisy! As a group, they cry out for Diversity but vote Monolithically!

How could the NAACP take a man like G.W. Busch and for politically motivated purposes, attempt to degrade him in the most vicious of ways! To associate him with what happened to Mr. Byrd, in any way, to those low-life, who actually perpetrated the crime against Mr. Byrd, was to say the least, a "Cheap-shot" The people who committed that heinous crime were properly punished and to the full extent of the law. This was a political move and a mean and vicious attempt by an organization supposedly meant to bring equal Justice to all, one has to ask—how could they stoop so low! What is really sickening about this fact is that the NAACP NEVER DISAVOWED THEIR COMPLICITY IN THE MAKING OF

SUBJECT COMMERICAL OR EVEN CLAIMED THEY REGRETED THE ATTEMPTED ASSOCIATION. Civil rights hell—they were attempting to assure more civil disorder!

Such a dastardly act can only be attributed to persons of the lowest moral character. One could ask the NAACP just what was so Civil about such and attempt to deceive their Voters. How could anyone with any sense of decency make such an outlandish and Despicable charge, a charge that was an out an out lie. Black or White—such an act could only be made by sick minds. And to have it, the commercial, run on national TV was evidence of their disgraceful disregard for the future characterization of there Organization. They, the blacks, claim that a "Mind is a terrible thing to waste." And They just proved their point!

HAS THE NAACP BECOME THE EMBODIMENT OF A CLASS OF OUR CITIZENS WHO ARE NO LONGER INTERESTED IN EQUAL RIGHTS but are more Interested in obtaining "Special Rights." As an organization, they are willing to tear there People down so the can build up their Political clout. Or, at least, they hope they will! Yes, their ancestors were sold into slavery by their own people and, to me; it looks like their present leaders, to their obvious detriment, are once again using them.

I am tired of my country, my race, being proclaimed as the "bogeyman" of the world. If you want to learn and know the facts as to what race has demonstrated the most cruelty to its people—you need only look to the nations of Africa. It is in the countries of Africa, past and present that has shown unbelievable cruelty toward its people. This can be born out by the history of these nations, down through the ages. Yes your ancestors came here as slaves, had they remained in Africa, they would not have survived long enough to have children. It is because of their coming to this land, as slaves, that you, the present day citizens, have come to know the advantages gained, by being born in this country. One could even say that, for the slaves sold to nations outside Africa it was for many of them, a life saving thing.

African nations from Ethiopia to the Sudan and in just about every other African country, the killings, tortures and rapes by fellow country men/women continues to this day. We, in American, know these facts cannot be denied. Still, it is the NAACP and others of the black leadership, who are trying to blame the white race, as usual, for all their problems. Continuing, as well, to paint the white citizens of this nation as the ones who are mean and cruel! Lets look at the facts:

1. America Cares (AmeriCares) battles HIV/Aids in Africa. Also, it was this organization that helped drought stricken Ethiopia.
2. Plant Hope in Haiti, consisting primarily of Americacares volunteers that provided seeds and small hand tools to farmers within this nation.

As a matter of fact, the history of this nation and its people is replete with stories of the goodness of our people. Still many black groups are preaching there mean spirited, self-serving trash talk and lies. Never mind that this nation has done more for the welfare of the black people throughout the world—than the majority of the nations throughout the world—including the United Nations (UN). Suggestion—get informed.

Today, we are being besieged with the outcries of many of our citizens—for Diversity. IT IS ONLY AFTER 9/11 THAT THESE CRIES HAVE BEEN SILENCED—AT LEAST TEMPORARIRLY. Under the guise of diversity and multiculturalism, we were, as a people, as a nation, being divided. Make no bones about it; the cry was not for unity, but for fragmentation of our society into special groups, each with their self-serving agenda. It was the old rational of "Divide and Conquer" being espoused and, in many cases, imposed on us. And, until recently, they seemed to be winning in their quest to split our people apart.

We the people. As a nation, must never forget that our accomplishments are unsurpassed and that they were made by virtue of our UNITY. As Michiale Barone in his recent book "The New Americans" points out, our most important issue is:

How too make our national motto "Out of many one" a living reality! To me, his book is a must read for every citizen that loves his country! On our nations capital is, as a part of the dome, a circle of pillars, which is symbolic of our national unity. Á "Circle of Unity" representing a united people.

This nation achieved its greatness not as a divided citizenship but by the molding of our people into one; hence we are known as the United States of America and not the Divided States of America. It is often stated that the genius of this country is of its "Melting Pot" and the coming together of it people—one nation under God, with Liberty and Justice for all. We must never forget that the essence of our "Unity" is in the Assimilation of our citizens of all nationalities, creeds and colors. We were not born out of division, a division that would, if it had been allowed to ferment, been the bitter fruit that would have divided us. Still there are those that would continually seek to divide us. When you hear the word diversity, the next word that should come to your mind is Perversity—for that is what it really is. Remember, "Unity" has always worked for us—Never forget it!

> "I have no passion for equality, which seems to me merely idealizing envy." Oliver Wendell Holmes.

Chapter XI

Poor vs. the Rich

We live in a capitalist society, we are a productive people and in general, we compliment each other. Without the workers, the businesses and the corporations working together we could not have produced the economic conditions that this nation has excelled in. No other nation on the face of this planet can, within its own borders, ever compete, one on one with us. Working together, in harmony, we have made the United States of America the most productive and prosperous country in the world.

It is by a simple formula that this Nation has come so far in such a, relatively speaking, short span of time. The formula was to make our Industrial Complex competitive and prosperous and the American wage earners some of the highest paid/compensated workers known, heretofore, to mankind!

Unlike many countries around the world that are divided by a two tier economic system—the poor and the rich—we live in a three-tier society and, in this way we have triumphed over other nations. We must always remain a three-dimensional society, for that is what has allowed us to become such a prosperous country.

Utopia is a dream, equality in all things is a dream that, if ever achieved, would soon become a nightmare. If we all, suddenly, become equal—who would be the worker, the leader and so on? Total equality may be a goal, it can never be6come a fact of life!

So what is the attraction of the blacks to liberalism. I think it can be found in there political leaderships, socialistic/ communistic agenda. To support my contention, we must look to the year 1898, when there was a split in the Democratic party and, as a consequence, this split, resulted in the formation of the Social Democratic Party of the United States of America.

With its formation and in its first convention, they affirmed their principals of Inter-National Socialism and contest with working class and the capitalist classes for the possession of powers of government and to use these powers to achieve their goals.

Stated in their thinking was "…the natural order of economic development that has separated society into the two antagonistic classes—the capitalist, a comparatively small class, the possessor of all the means of production and distribution…and the large and ever increasing class of wage workers possessing no means of production." From this we can see, from its inception, this party was hell bent on class warfare to achieve there goals, playing class against class, and in the realities of today, race against race. In this respect, in their preamble they state:

> We therefore, call upon the wageworkers of the United States, without distinctions of color, race, sex or creed, and upon all citizens in sympathy with the historic mission of the working class, to organize under the banner of the Social Democratic Party, as a party truly representing the interest of the toiling masses and uncompromisingly waging war upon the exploiting class, until the system of wage slavery shall be abolished and the Co-Operative Commonwealth established.

Immediate Demands

As steps in that direction, we make the following demands:

First —   Revision of our federal constitution, in order to remove the obstacles to complete control of Governments irrespective of race, creed or sex.

Second — The public ownership of all industries controlled by monopolies, trusts, and combines.

Third — The public ownership of all railroads, telegraphs, and telephones; all water-works, gas and electric plants and public utilities.

Fourth — The public ownership of all gold, silver, copper, lead, iron, coal, and other mines, and all oil and gas wells.

Fifth — The reduction of the hours of labor in proportion to increasing facilities of production.

Sixth — The inauguration of a system of public works and improvements for the employment of the unemployed, the public credits to be utilized for that purpose.

Seventh— Useful inventions to be free, the inventors to be remunerated by the public/

Eight — Labor legislation to be National, instead of local, and international when possible.

Ninth — National insurance of working people against accidents, lack of employment, and want in old age.

Tenth — Equal civic and political rights for men and women, and the abolition of all laws discriminating against women.

Eleventh— The adoption of the initiative and referendum, proportional representation, and the right of recall or representatives by the voters.

Twelfth — Abolition of war and the introductions of international arbitration.

Today, much of what was outlined in subject manifesto has come to pass. The Democratic Parties present-day constituency, obviously wildly accepts what has, thus far. happened. What is left to come will be, if it should come to pass, destructive to our people and as well, our nation. we, through liberalism and Political Correctness have lost all personal perspective. We have allowed ourselves to, like it or not, participate in our nations subjugation to those that would turn us into a socialistic society at the least and for the most, a Communistic Nation.

Despite the evidential evidence throughout the world; that communistic forms of government have proven to be total failures and a monumental relic of the past. Still, within our society, there are those unwilling to face the truth evident by the numerous facts, attesting to its failure, that surrounds all of us. Yes, it is still appropriate to remind ourselves of the fact that "What fools we Mortals are."

This nation and its people must be ever vigilant and weary to this possibility. For it could come to past—leading to the destruction of our nation, as we know it. Soon the founders and builder of this nation will become a minority race in their own country. No other nation or people would allow this to happen. Yet, it is about to happen in our country. One can rightly ask, how is it that we have allowed this to happen— could it be the result of the divide and conquer mentality prevalent throughout our nation. How could we have stood by and allowed it to happen? Will history look on us, in the future, as buffoons—a class of people that, in their ignorance, lost its majority to the minorities?

I cannot recall, in history, any other nation that has so succumbed to the will of others and in so doing, forfeited their country to them, without a shot being fired in defense of our heritage our country.

I am not the only one who is aware of what is taking place in our society. As an example; Balint Vazsonyi, a Hungarian born historian, drawing on his personal first hand Knowledge, in his book "America's 30 Years War," describes how our hard-won freedoms are gradually being eroded and makes a powerful case that America is going down the road to an authoritarian regime (Government).

> "...Customarily, the opening salvo of the battle
> is to postulate that an American identity does not
> exist. Our strength, the suggestions goes is in
> our diversity."

56

"As the case with "social justice" and all it's diversity, no explanation—much less a definition—exists of the word "diversity." All we are told is that diversity is good."

The above, in essence, supports my contention that we are being used and abused, as a people as a nation, by the use of words! As pointed out and questioned; just what is the meaning of these words: Diversity, Social Justice and such?" It now appears that we have unwittingly let those that would supplant our values to theirs, deceive us! Yes they have defined the meaning of these words to mean what 'they' say they mean. Like blind sheep, we have accepted their definitions.

I have been saying this for years. There is no such thing as an African—American; no more so than there is an African-Italian, African-German. If you are born in America, you are plain and simple—an America. What's wrong with that? Why do the black citizens of this country desire or even feel it necessary to be so identified. It is obviously a ploy, in my opinion, to set the races apart. We are a nation of many nationalities and I must say, that among the various nationalities, the blacks would be the least to need to separate themselves! Is it just a tool to further separate their race? One can only guess! Could it be for such things as affirmative action, quotas and such. Do you every wonder how it is that they are considered our peers for Jury duty, but not for going to college? Now, more then ever, instead of separating themselves by race or color, they need to assimilate and become a part of our total citizenship.

Or is it possible that their leadership has a separate goal for their race. Is the "New Black Panters," in fact, a display of armed power and a threat to the other races? I find this hard to believe and frankly, I don't! Still I must question why separatism seems to be a part of their goal.

Today, many black groups, such as the Panthers have, over the years, formed themselves Into armed groups. But when the whites formed militia groups, throughout this nation, they came under strict scrutiny and harsh criticism not only from the black leaders of this nation, but also our Politicos as well. Particularly those officials that would disarm us and take away our Second Amendment Rights. And guess what, far to many whites, in their ignorance, are all for gun control, ignoring the fact that it is not the honest citizens of this nation that they need to be weary of. This display of ignorance, I fear, could come back to hunt us.

In his book: "Hating Whitey" Mr. Horowitz points out the following cliché of the left: "White people only respond to blacks when they have a gun to their heads." Think about it!

Many OF our citizens, black and white alike, are all too willing to jump on the backs of the rich claiming that they have too much and must willingly share their wealth. They have to be either ignorant or just plain stupid. Don't they know the rich need money to employ others. When was the last time they went to work for nothing. Without the rich—who would employ them? Without the rich there would be no middle class. As previously noted, there are many two Tier SOCIETIES—they are called "Third World COUNTRIES." The African people are a major part of the poor people why, because they do not have enough rich people in their countries, to give them jobs.

In American today, there are still those that take great satisfaction in their efforts to berate us as a race and a country. They are "of little self-worth," having accomplished little in their own right, they now look to find only the bad in others and in our country.

The only way they can find solace is by putting others down. They don't dislike the rich, They hate them! Unfortunately there will always be a certain number of this ilk within every Society.

They, rightly so, are called Freeloaders! So when you find a person that has nothing good to say about the rich or his country, you can quickly discern that he/she is a Pimp—one who lives off the earnings of others—particularly the Taxpayers?

"There isn't such a reasonable fellow in the world, to hear him talk. He never wants anything but what's right and fair, only when you come to settle what's right and fair, it's everything he wants? and nothing that you want. And that's his idea of compromise (fairness). Thomas Hughes.

Chapter XII

Black-Blue, Guns and the Media

In his book "When Nations Die" by Jim Nelson Black, published by Tyndale Publishers, Inc., he makes, in part, the following comments: "Violence, hatred, and rage flame out of control in our cities and towns of today. And under benign-sounding names as "choice, "free speech," and "Liberation," we permit hotheads and radicals to make a mockery of sacred landmarks and Institutions as old as the nation itself. The atmosphere of permissiveness, in turn, threatens our survival as a nation.

Earlier, in this book, I discussed in some detail, the situation that had only recently occurred in the city of Cincinnati, Ohio. Now about three months later, at the time of this writing, a much different situation is taking place in that city. Instead of condemning, protesting and rioting against the Police of that city for shooting a black man, one of 15 that were killed by the Police during the past five years; it seems that the chickens have come home to roost. Finally, the Police had enough and decided to take matters, so to speak, into their own hands. How, by some internal consensus, I guess, among the policemen of all colors, they initiated a temporary "hands off" approach to crime; thereby making a strong statement to the community: That you asked for it and finally, you got it— minimum lawful intervention by the law enforcement officers.

As a result the city of Cincinnati soon became a heaven for Criminal activity. In just a little over three months, there were, as I understand it, 90 black on black crimes—resulting in many killings. What is strange about this is that little of this civil disorder was reported in the national media; nor was there any rioting in the streets, in outrage, concerning the number of blacks that were being killed by blacks. This time, the whites could not be blamed! I guess if a cop kills one, a black, it is riot and protest time, however, if they, the blacks kill each other in a massive crime spree—hell, that's just fine!

What is the message that the blacks are sending to us? The message is that they can kill their own, as often and as many as they want to. In short the killing of black s is all right as long as they do it. If a Police Officer kills one in the execution of his duties, it is party time (rioting) in the streets. In this manner, they feel free to complain and, in fact, that they are justified in running wild in the streets, stealing, destroying and yes, breaking the law. If anyone is stupid enough to think that when the blacks take to the street and riots, it is in protest to the death of one of them—you have to be out of your mind!

It is noted that many of the black on black killings referred to, were with guns. I wonder, has gun control laws, in these cases, demonstrated that when enforced only against the lawful citizens, and not enforced against the criminals, such laws are a shame and only prove that our gun control laws are ineffective and a total failure—at least in the inner cities. Why is it that the Liberal media, and the black, self-anointed "Deputy-Dwags, such as Jesse and Big Al are not in the streets when blacks are killing blacks in massive numbers. At times like this where is all their screaming, hollering, and so on. Oh, I forget, it's ok for blacks to kill blacks, or at least it appears to be so. Recently Big Al said, in essence: "Because he got your skin, he isn't your kin." It seems like, in cases of this nature, he knows what he is talking about.

If this many children, black or white, were killed in a school shooting, and in such a short time frame; the media would be all over the situation—blaming not the kids, but the guns. Today, we have in the majority, a Liberal Press, crying for their First Amendments rights, while they continue to attack our citizens Second Amendment rights. Talk about fairness in the media. They are in fact, one of the largest groups of hypocrites, in the entire nation; exceeded in Numbers only by the PC CROWD.

If your reading, listening, or watching TV, you are witnessing, that while crime on the streets is ever increasing, these liberal dispatchers of lies and excuses for the criminals, are reporting that the reason for the massive number of crimes being committed, is because to many guns are in the hands of our honest citizens. Yes, these liberal dispatchers of lies—the supposedly free press—have, over the past many years, distorted what is really taking place in our country. How? By making the gun, in the hands of our law-abiding citizens, the culprit instead of the criminals now running amuck in certain cities in our nation. If gun control, as being Imposed on honest people is the answer, how come it's not working in cities such as Cincinnati. I thought the Brady Bill was suppose to take guns out of the hands of these hoodlums. Instead, it appears that the Brady Bill has served only to pre-occupy the police with checking to insure that only honest citizens abide by gun-control-laws. And guess what, a great many of our citizens have fallen for this line of media "PC-BS" hook line and sinker!

To this date, in their ignorance, the oft-repeated chant that guns are made to kill is still being shouted out, loud and clear, even by those who should know better! Why is this? Well for those that cannot think for themselves, it is because the liberal press/media has drummed the idea that guns are the fault—not the one wielding the gun!

What is the t truth about guns? Are they only made to kill? In his book, "The Story of the Gun," by Ivan V. Hogg and published by A&E books, St. Martin's Press. He makes the following statements:

> "Like it or not, the gun has made the world what it is today. It has determined national boundaries, determined types of government, fed millions of people and protects millions more from predatory animals. True, it has killed tens of millions of people, but it must be remembered that people were killing each other long before the gun appeared on the scene, and if every gun vanished from the face of the earth tomorrow, people would still find ways to kill each other."

What the liberal media does not tell their followers is that the majority of the killings, with guns are not in white schools, as they would have you to believe, but in inner city black ghettoes as well as in the Hispanic neighborhoods, throughout the land. Relatively speaking, in the America of today, blacks are killing blacks—with guns—in unprecedented numbers. As a group, they are unsurpassed in killing their own. For example, in our nations capitol, the black children are killing each other at an unbelievable rate, still you won't find much news, regarding this fact, in the liberal News media.

In South Africa, with the ending of Apartheid, and as well in Zimbabwe hundreds, if not thousands of blacks are slaughtering the white farmers and their families. In South Africa, the killing of whites has increased dramatically—however we seem not to hear or read much about this fact. For some reason, the liberal media is not interested in this part of the world any longer. I wonder why? Not only that, it is now a fact that the importation of cheap American made guns, are being purchased, in great numbers, within African Nations. Again, why do we not find much about this matter, in the new media? Could it be that the only interest they have in gun control is in trying to disarm the law abiding citizens of this nation?

Down through history, denying the citizens arms to defend themselves has only worked to the detriment of a free society. Hitler, as well as others of his ilk, knew this truth all to well. It is only among the ill informed within our society, or among the uneducated, that we can find many of our citizens, unwilling to or incapable of comprehending this fact.

> "If one man can be allowed to determine for himself what is law, every man can. That means first chaos then tyranny. Legal process is an essential part of the democratic process." Justice Felix Frankfurter.

Chapter XIII

Racial Blackmail

Today the Black Leadership within this country is attacking our nation and the corporations of the country. Have no doubt about it, the black extortionists are, for all practical purposes, harassing our Corporations—the basic ingredient in a Capitalistic Society.

It is my opinion that the Jesse Jackson's and Al Sharpton's, coupled with what it appears to be; the approval of the NAACP; are using the "Boycott" as a tool—their hammer—to subjugate our Corporate Chief Executive Officers (CEO's) to crumble at their feet. This display of weakness in our corporate leadership is disgusting and should not be tolerated by their Stock holders. They need to be taken to task and told in plain English, if they cave into any treat by blackmailers, from any quarter, the will be, voted out of their job. Weakness in the face of the enemy, let alone a Blackmailer, cannot be tolerated.

So how has is it that the liberal black leadership of this nation, from any quarter can, arbitrarily, face down our Corporations and threaten them with a boycott? Has the use of a Boycott becomes a tool, an instrument to legitimize blackmail? Today, one can truly say that the term "Blackmail" has been given some credence by the black leadership.

What is a boycott? According to the Dictionary, it is: boycott v. & n. 1. Combine in refusing Social or commercial relations with a person, group, country etc.) Usu. As punishment or Coercion...also the word "Blacklist" is indicated as a verb!

What is the meaning of the term/word Blackmail. Among other meanings it is, according to the Dictionary: Blackmail n. & v. 1. n. an extortion of payment in return for...v. tr. 1. Extort or try to Extort money by blackmail.

At least by definition, and in my opinion, the black leadership, across this nation is heavily involved in extorting and or blackmailing our companies as well as many businesses. My question, why are so many of our nations

CEO's caving into this out and out extortion or at the very least, neo-extortionist now pervasive within this nation by one particular race of people. Paying anything to anyone, under the threat of any kind; seems, to me, to be illegal. No I am not a lawyer, however there are times when reason should prevail. We cannot let any single group take advantage over any part of this nation in general, or any reason!

We know that in many instances, the black leadership uses the threat of boycott. Remember, every black not entitled, but hired under the treat of a black boycott, are gaining advantage over others and perhaps, even displacing someone of another race. This cannot be tolerated. If we are all equal we should all be equally treated in the work place. No group or individual should be advanced based on a threat, opposed to individual merit.

The CEO's that are giving into this form of extortion/blackmail are cowards and should not be in charge of anything. The way things are going, the Conjunctive CEO could rightly have a true meaning as "COWARDS EACH ONE." The shareholders/stockholders of this nation must rise to the occasion and prohibit the payment, under the treat of blackmail by boycott, to anyone; without first having a Stock/Share holders meeting to gain their approval. After all it is your money that they are giving to these damnable blackmailers. In my humble opinion, those who would use extortionist tactics, to gain advantage of any sort, are the lowest form of humanity.

It is about time that the productive part of this nation to stand-up and be counted. Not one more dimes should be given. If money is to be exchanged in manners of this nature, it should be exchanged in the Courts of this nation—not in any back office deals.

Who are they, these blackmailers, to feel that they have the right to determine whom, what color and how many of their race should be hired based solely on the color of their skin. The blacks of this nation, that I have come to know, can and will stand on their own two feet. It is their leadership that lacks the backbone to do that—no they must first downgrade the intelligence of their own people by proclaiming that without the likes of them, the blacks cannot make it on their own!

I am sick of hearing how, in the past, they have been deprived—deprived of what. The blacks are better off in this nation, then they would be in any other country. However, for some, it appears that they will ride the dark horse of the past—slavery—as long as they can. Equal rights has, to some blacks, become exploitation of ones rights against another, for personal advantage. And they are getting away with!

It seems, in many cases and situations, the other races of this nation are having their rights subordinated to the rights of the blacks. Such as in the job market, our educational system and yes in our rights to free speech. Today the blacks freely use the dreaded "N" word amongst each other—but let no one else dare to do so! My question: what gives them the right to deny the use of this word to any other? For the information of the ill or uninformed—the word "nigger" is in our Dictionaries. What right has any race any group to deny to the citizens of this nation, the use of? Any word. A word that has several meanings, is our right to use it in any of its form and not Conditioned on their approval. If so—who gave them this right? I do not understand how a race of people could be given exclusive rights to a word, based only on what they conceive its meaning to be! Only recently a book titled "Nigger" written by a black legal scholar has been published. I think that is great. I understand that, even among the blacks, this word has various meanings and yes some meanings are enduring. If it hurts some, lets get it out in the open and find out just how it affects them.

How is it that the "RAPPERS" can freely and all to frequently use the "N" word. How can any Race or group hold sway over others in the matter of free usage of the language, as defined in the dictionary. It is only by its general usage, can a word be defined—not by those would silence the use of it, a word, because somehow it hurts their feelings. I have been called many words—words not pleasing to me ears; however, I do not feel I have the right to forbid anyone to use such words.

Yes, this word, in some form of usage, could be offensive. But so could many others! To me this word, offensive to some, has no overriding meaning that would disallow its use by any race. If the blacks can use It, to describe another black—its use should not be denied to the other races. IF IT IS A PART OF SPEECH ITS USAGE BY OTHERS SHOUOLD NOT BE ARBITRARILY DISALLOWED BASED ONLY ON THE FACT THAT IT OFFENDS!

There is an old saying that "sticks and stones may break my bones but names can never hurt me". Are blacks the only ones to be exempted from name-calling and degrading words?

Along this line, I suggest that a more inappropriate term, all to frequently use by blacks is the "MF" word. I cannot find it in any of my dictionaries. Why do black "RAPPERS" commonly use it? Especially in the black communities and. In fact, if the rappers were denied the use of this Word(s), they would be left speechless. I know that this term is abhorred by many and in all communities. It is a vile and disgusting use of the English language and should not be used—Period! However, its usage by blacks has become so prevalent that if a child says the word "MOTHER," THEY THINK HE ONLY KNOWS HALF A WORD!

In a way, prohibiting the use of the "N" word is scratching for another reason to divide us and perhaps even sue us, one the grounds of racial discrimination or whatever! In fact, I wonder "does thou protest to loudly."

> "Without freedom of thought, there can be no such thing as wisdom; and no such thing as public Liberty without freedom of speech." Benjamin Franklin.

Chapter XIV

Flags and there Abuse

For years now, this nation, because of a liberal Supreme court that allowed our National Flag to be treated in every despicable way possible and with impunity. How is it that only recently we have learned that at least several blacks, in high places and perhaps many others are, in effect, saying that they "owe no allegiance to this nations flag, Old Glory" and, by implication, to the country for which it stands, The United States of America. Now it appears that Al Sharpton, in a recent speech to an all black audience, proclaimed that the black of this nation owe this country nothing. I guess by his remarks, this would include loyalty.

During the past several years, in addition to our national flag, the Confederate flag—which played a major roll in our nations history and heritage—has also been under attack. Unfortunately, these attacks have, directed by the NAACP, been effectively made, preventing this flag from being displayed over such places as State Capitols and other public places. Why has this been allowed to happen? Well, in my opinion this was allowed to happen because, once again, cowardice in our elected officials. It is only recently that the blacks are, saying, that the sight of it, the confederated flag, hurts their feelings. And of course, in a liberal "Political Correct Society," the bleeding hearts have once again prevailed. Also it should be noted that the blacks did not feel this way until the NAACP TOLD THEM TO!

Still, I wonder how the flags under which they have been raised, can be offensives, while the Flags of the very nations that sold them into slavery—that fly over the United Nation Building and many African Embassies are not also offensive to them! Could it be that the African nations or the U.N. would tell them where they could "stick it," their bleeding hearts! How is it that many things about our history, that bothers them, are only now being addressed? Could these issues be manufactured ones, so as to enhance a political or organizational motivated agenda?

Recently, in her apparent stupidity, a black female and state representative claimed that she would not pledge allegiance to any flag (meaning our nations flag) that flew over the "Colonies" at a time when slavery was being tolerated in America. Talk about a dumb remark, a remark that causes one to wonder how she ever got elected to such a high office within a state. Her lack of knowledge, in respect to our nations flag, is inexcusable! Her ignorance of this nations history leaves much to be desired. Perhaps she is only interested in tearing it, our nation, down as opposed to her boning up on the history of a country that has so greatly enriched her. For her enlightenment, the America Flag never flew over any of the American Colonies. The flag was not even designed or made until after the signing of the Declaration of Independence and the Revolutionary War when we became a Nation, that our National Flag was Flow, not over the Colonies, but over the United States of America.

As noted in the "World ALMANAC," The Civil War, I861-65 grew out of sectional disputes over the continued existence of slavery in the South and the Southern Legislation that states maintain many sovereign rights...It should, further, be noted that the Civil War evolved out of two distinct points of contention—slavery as well as states rights. Unfortunately second point point, by the black protesters are, for advantage, almost always overlooked. To this date, for many blacks, the Civil War was only fought because of slavery. Apparently many whites are also ignorant of the fact that for many "States Rights" was the issue. In fact, General Lee never believed in slavery and States rights were his sole concern when accepting the Generalship of the Confederate Army. Should he now be dishonored for his beliefs!

To appease the black leadership, regarding the confederate flag was to deny to the whites, a part of their heritage and yes, their honor. The great, great majority of the Confederate army consisted of young and very poor men. None of them ever owed a plantation much less a slave. Again, through ignorance, a great part of our citizenship is being held hostage for the acts of, relatively speaking, few citizens of that time!

Although born in the State of Illinois, the land of Lincoln, I feel that even old "Abe" would oppose these many attempts t o now vilify the sacrifices of those "young" men who died in defense of their cause. The Black Leadership, of recent years has, it seems to me, reviewed our nations past only to look for things they can "Bitch" about, primarily, to enhance and enrich there position and their wealth. Yes there are those among the black leaders, who would do anything, attempt anything that could lead to destroying this nations history. Only by pulling this nation down, could they hope to lift themselves up in the eyes of their followers. However, it is also the fault of some of the souths, supposed leaders, who have shown themselves to be cowards in defense of all things—States Rights. This should make their forefathers really proud of them?

Once again, and only recently, in this nations House of Representative, the right to attack our National flag was called into question. Watching the debates being waged on the floor of the House of Representatives was, to say the least, disappointing and at times, downright maddening! Particular as to how so many of the peoples representatives, both black and white, that was opposed to the Amendment drawn to protect our national flag. Their lack of concern for our nations number one symbolism is as to what we are, as a nation, all about. To have to listen to so much ignorance, at one time, was disgusting! After 9/11, I can guarantee you that none of those, making disparaging remarks on the floor of the House, would now dare to repeat their words in the climate of today.

More than ever, our citizenship has turned to our flag as a symbol of our nations honor and glory—loved by the majority, disrespected by a few but, to all, a rallying point by which we can gather around in defense of our people as well as our nation. Today, as always, our nations Flag has served us well. My question: How can anyone, knowing the history of our flag, not rise to defend it. How can they pledge allegiance to it, almost daily, but show no allegiance to it when It counts? Are they willing to say to these brave men; those that fought and died for what our flag represents, that it is only a rag, a piece of cloth, one that can be sown disrespect by those who have no respect for it. IS THIS THE TYPE OF LEADERSHIP WE INTENTIONALLY ELECTED OR WANT? For our nation, our citizens, and our flag—I hope not!

As of 9/11, honoring our flag, by all our citizens, of every race, creed and color has once again, taken hold. Yes, as a nation, as a people—all AMERICANS, we have united. The Amendment to protect our flag passed in the House of Representatives, in a bi-partisan Vote. It has still to pass in the Senate.

Regarding this matter, there was a speech on the floor of the House that I feel is worthy of special note:

H.J. Res. 36

Flag Protection Constitutional Amendment
Remarks by
Honorable Henry Hyde

We look around this chamber and we see the splendid diversity of America, we see men and women whose great-grandparents come from virtually every corner of the globe. What holds this democratic community together? A common commitment to certain moral norms is the foundation of the democratic experiment.

Human beings don't live by abstract ideas alone. Those ideas are embodied in symbols. And what is a symbol? A symbol is much more than a sign. A sign simple conveys some information. A symbol is much more richly textured. A symbol is material reality that makes a spiritual reality present among us. An octagonal piece of red metal on a street corner is a "sign." The flag is a symbol. Vandalizing a "No Parking" sign is a misdemeanor, but burning the flag is a hate crime, because burning the flag is an expression of contempt for the moral unity of the American people that the flag symbolically makes present to us. Every day.

Why do we need this amendment now? Is there a rash of flag burning going on? No, happily there is not, but I believe we live in a time of growing disunity—our society is pulled apart by the powerful centrifugal force of racism, ethnicity, language, culture, gender and religion.   Diversity can be a source of strength, but disunity is a source of peril. If you stop and think, the world is torn by religions and ethnic divisions that make war and killing and death and terror the norm in so many countries—Ireland, the Middle East, the Balkans, Rwanda—look around the globe and see what hate can do to drive fellow human beings apart.

This legislation makes a statement that needs to be made—our flag is the transcendent symbol of all that America stands for and aspires to be and hence deserves the special protection of the law.

We Americans share a moral unity, expressed so profoundly in country's birth certificate, the Declaration of Independence, "We hold these truths to be self-evident..." Jefferson wrote. The 'truth' that the right to life and liberty is inalienable and inviolable.   The 'truth' that government is intended to facilitate and not impede the people's pursuit of happiness.

Adherence to these truths is the foundation of civil society, of democratic culture in America. And what is the symbol of our moral unity amidst our racial, ethnic and religious diversity. The flag...Old Glory...The Stars and Stripes.

In seeking to provide constitutional protection for the flag, we are seeking to protect the moral unity that makes American democracy possible. We have spent the better part of the last thirty years or so telling each other all the things that divide us. It is time to start talking about the things that units us—that makes us all, together, Amer4icans.   The flag is the embodiment of the unit of the American people, a unity built on these "self-evident" truths on which the American experiment rests—the truths, which are our nation's claim to be a just society.

Let us take a step toward reconciliation—and toward constitutional sanity—by adopting the amendment. The flag is our connection to the past and proclaims our hopes and aspirations for the future.

Too many brave American have marched behind it—too many have come home in a box covered by a flag—too many parents and widows have clutched that to their hearts as the last remembrance of the beloved one to treat that flag with anything less than reverence and respect. About 187 years ago during the British bombardment of Baltimore, Frances Scott key looked towards Fort McHenry in the early dawn, and asked his famous question—

To his joy, he saw our flag was still there—and how surprised would he be to learn our flag is even planted on the moon!

But—most especially—it is implanted in the hearts pf every loyal American.

This rendering represents an outstanding statement as to just what our country and our flag means to us; or should mean to each and every one of us. I, particularly, am pleased with the ending that points out—distinctively "...every 'Loyal' American.

> "The time has come when those sentiments should be uttered and if it is decreed that I should go down because of this speech, then let me go down linked with the truth—let me die in the Advocacy of what is just and right." Abraham Lincoln.

Chapter XV

No Silver Spoons

Today, there is among many, a belief that all white men/women are born rich. Yes, to them, we have had it made throughout our lives—from cradle to the grave—the white race consists of only the rich! To dispel this notion, this self-serving belief and for once and for all, put this "Hogwash" to rest, I am relating a part of my childhood life; a life-style that millions upon millions had to endure during the years of the Great Depression and for some through the years of World War II.

Also, in a way, I am using this chapter to pay tribute to a great lady, who I was fortunate enough to have her play a roll in my younger life and upbringing:

I was born the middle child, one of eleven children in Joliet, Illinois, November 27, 1930. My ancestry was, on my fathers side—Croatian and on my mothers side Slovenian. I am an American. As many would know, the year of my birth was only the second year of the Depression. My father, because of his limited education coupled with the depressed job market, could only find minimal type work, primarily working for the Works Project Administration (WPA). My mother, an epileptic, could not work outside the home or, for that matter, because of her health, do very little in the home.

During most of my childhood I, along with the rest of the family, lived in what could only be described as abject poverty. (I frequently say that my black and Mexican friends only hung around with me, so that they could have someone to look down on.) By todays standard, we would have been considered the poorest of the poor.

For the greatest part of this period, my family was on "Relief." (In today's vernacular we were on Welfare). I make no apology for this, my father worked hard, six days a week, with pick and shovel, for the WPA, We had no food stamps and gratefully accepted dried beans, dried fruits, cereals, oleomargarine, flour, powdered milk and such. To supplement these meager rations, my older brothers and I would, for extra food, occasionally pick rotten fruits from garbage cans behind a grocery store. My mother could cut the good parts out for us to eat, so that we had, from time to time, fresh fruit to eat.

Many a night we had to sit by the coal/wood-burning stove, waiting until the bread being baked was ready to come out of the oven. At times like this, and on many occasions, this would be all we had to eat. If lucky, we had some sugar or "oleo" to put on our bread. If we were really lucky, we had both!

The houses we lived in, for the most part, were "Rat-Traps." We moved in and tired to make them livable. Today, many on welfare move into good/new public hosing and, in short order, they are turned into Rat-Houses. Our clothing primarily consisted of hand-me-downs, or ones that we could get from the relief agency, which in turn, eventually became our hand me downs. As soon as we could, we earned a little money by selling newspapers, shinning shoes and such. As we grew older, we got better jobs, such as, working in a Bowling alley, for the Junk-man and on various other jobs.

Although my mother was an epileptic, we received no government health benefits. For the most part, my mother's health care was provided by her doctor—free gratis. We did not have, nor could we afford health insurance? If we got sick, we had to learn to though/sweat it out. Local Home remedies were, in fact, the main source of our health care. My father was our Barber, Dentist, Shoemaker and whatever the situation called for. Still we survived! One thing for sure, we were not proud of our life-style, even hating to admit to anyone that we were on relief. We did not voluntarily choose to live on—what little there was—relief. We were poor, and my father did the best he could in providing for his family. We wanted to get off relief—not live off it.

During the Depression years, out of a total national population of 120,000.000 the unemployment rate we 29 percent of the population. The largest employer was the government—the WPA. The hourly wage paid was 30 cents per-hour. Still, from time to time, my dad would find other work, even if it was only for a short while. The reason he could find these jobs is because he was willing to work and was a good worker! He was a proud man, he did not wish to beholden to anyone. However, circumstances dictated his life—he had little choice.

Yes, I am proud of my father as well as the rest of the family. We did not play the "poor me" or the "blame game," back then, there was no time for self-pity. We played the hand that was dealt us and got on with it. Not only my family but millions of others, as well!

Today, with inner pride, I can say that I was a child of the Depressions years. I am proud of this fact and the people of this great country, of all races, creeds and colors, who did not give up during this very trying period in our nations History.

Yes, they were poor, but they were proud and with love of country and a willingness to work when and where they could find it. They had no minimum wage, except when working for the WPA, when the minimum was also the maximum. Even when they could not find regular work—they some how found ways to get by.

In my humble opinion we were a nation of people with great pride and personal character. I am sorry that in this current day and age, we can no longer make this claim!

In the "Great Society Years" we find that amongst us, there are many people, recipients of this program, that has come to believe that government owes them a living. The truth of the matter is that people of all races and from time to time have needed some form of help and for the most part, and in one-way or another it was provided. However, no one deserves a free ride!

When it comes to being poor, all races have had an "equal opportunity, to be/become so! The clue to not being poor is to work you way out of it, as the great majority of our people have.

Today we have a certain group amongst us that feel they are entitled to a certain amount of money per hour. This would be fine, if they would also willingly work hard enough to earn that amount of money. In short, you should be paid according to what you produce. You produce little—you earn little. A loafer is not worth the value of a producer. Today, by government degree interjected into the free market system, they have assumed the right to determine what a man should be paid and not by what he earns!

How about "ask not what your employer can do for you but what you can do for your employer" Wages or standards of wages should not be a gift or an entitlement. One should be paid according to his worth. There should be no equality in the work place—the one who works should be paid according to his value to the company—not what some distant politicians determines! This nation must return to established work ethnic standards.

Today, we have people who feel that if they just showed up, they are entitled to being paid. In this day and age, when our unemployment rate is low, an indication that jobs are available, we find many all to willing to live off the government—willing to become enslaved to government largess. Yes they are willing to take from the productive part of society, the taxpayers. They have yet to learn that there is no such thing as a free ride. Franklin D. Roosevelt, the father of the "New Deal" in his message to Congress, January 4, 1935, stated:

> "Continual dependence upon relief (Welfare) induces a spiritual and moral disintegration fundamentally destructive to the national fiber. To dole out relief in this way is to administer a narcotic, a subtle destroyer of the human spirit."

To this day, the liberal Democrats will not heed the waning.

In regards to "Affirmative Action," I would like to relate this personal story of mine:

As pointed out earlier in this book, my mother was an epileptic and during part of the year's 1935-6, she had to be hospitalized. As a consequence our family was, temporarily broken up and the five oldest children, which included me, were sent to an Orphans home. My baby brother at this time, was to young to go to the Orphan's Home. He went to live with one of my mother's sisters and her family.

After about eight months, my Dad learned that my mother was being used to do janitorial work, much of the time, instead of getting the medical help/care she needed, so he took her out of the Hospital, rented a house and took us out of the Orphan's Home. It was following this that Mrs. Lewis (a black lady) came to our home. She was, as a part of the Relief program, provided to care for my mother and also keep house and care for us children. In short, she became our surrogate mother.

Coinciding with the arrival of Mrs. Lewis to our home was to be my first year of school. Because I was born in the month of November, I was almost seven when I became a first grader. The school I was to attend was a Catholic School, located across the river from where I lived and about two miles away. For me, it was a long walk. Sometime during the early part of my school year, a boy from my class confronted me during recess, calling me names and talking about how poorly I was dressed and so forth. As a result, we got into a fight. The Nun, who came upon this incident and without asking for my side of the story, sent me home from school. I cried all the way home, because I didn't think it was right to only blame me! When I got home and still crying, Mrs. Lewis asked what happened. After explaining everything to her she, without another word, put on her brown bowler type hat, took me by the hand and we walked, hand in hand, back across the Jackson Street river bridge to my school.

To this day, I don't know what she said to the Nun; however I was allowed, that day, to return to School. To this day, whenever I hear the words "Affirmative action" the aforementioned incident, involving Mrs. Lewis and I, comes to mind. By her resolute, she showed me what it means to be firm in ones actions. Also, it was long before Civil Rights, that Mrs. Lewis and I crossed that bridge. I think of her often and will love and remember her until the day I die. Note: Long after Mrs. Lewis left our family, while I was working on an Ice Truck, at age 13, during the war, she became one of my customers. Although I tried to give her free Ice—she would have none of that—she would accept charity of no kind.

In my mind she, Mrs. Lewis epitomizes many of the black people I have come, down through the years, to know and respect. Knowing her I think "REPARATIONS" would, if ever, be the last thing on her mind. She had too much self-respect.

> "We must beware of trying to build a society in which nobody counts for anything except a politician or an official, a society where enterprise gains no reward and thrift no privileges." Winston Churchill.

Chapter XVI

Racism in America

In his book "Race and Culture" Thomas Sowell (a renowned black professor) points out the following:

> "The biggest story about slavery—how this ancient institution older than either Islam or Christianity, was wiped out over vast regions of the earth remains a story seldom told. At the heart of the story was the West's ending slavery in its own domain within a century and maintaining pressure on other nations for even longer to stamp out this practice. Instead, the West has been singled out as peculiarly culpable for worldwide evil for which it participated, when in fact its only real uniqueness was in ultimately opposing and destroying this evil..."

In furtherance, I can only come to one conclusion and is that today, we now have a large part of one race of citizens, that in their opinion has, over the years been picked on and discriminated against by the white man. This, in part and at one time in our nations history could be rightly stated/believed. However, that time has long ended. It must now be put to rest.

Today, there is still racism but in fact, in today's world, racism is a two-way street. Yes there is still a lot of hatred for the white man by the blacks of this nation. It seems strange that some blacks will pay homage to those that first placed them in bondage—the nations of Africa! While, on the other hand, they tend to dishonor those people, the whites, that freed their people from the chains of slavery.

However, it has been well documented that it was the Arabic and African nations that first practice the enslavements of their own people. Yes, down through the centuries, these nations have dealt in slavery and to this day, within them, it still exists.

Also, and to this day, a little known fact exists, that is that in America, it was not only the whites who owned and participated in enslaving blacks—their own people—in this country. Yes blacks of this nation, the freeman, the northern blacks some of which, also had slaves. Question, will they be sorted out and required to pay reparations?

As previously noted, slavery in Africa was going on long before our nation came on the scene. Still there are m\those who are quick to blame the white man of this country while honoring those, the blacks of Africa that sold them into slavery. How, by choosing to be called African-Americans. This I cannot understand! Why do the pay homage to the ones that first enslaved them? How is it that they, many blacks, are so willing to blame the whites, yet have open arms for those who sold them on the world markets. I wonder, could it be that the whites in America have money, while the blacks of Africa don't. Is this hatred of the whites born out of a possibility that the black race could further enrich itself at the expense of the white man? Is this what a call for "Reparations" is all about?

Like many of you and you leaders I can, as well, go on pointing out the faults of your race. What good does it do, for either race to continue to berate the other? There is good and evil within all people. As Americans we must put aside those things that only seek to divide our people. Is some possible financial gain, worth the risk of destroying each other in a racial conflict? I think not!

By now, most of the people of the black race are aware that your race of people is the oldest on this planet. Yet, the nations of Africa are held out to be, for the most part. "Third World Countries."

Better stated, many nations of Africa are basically and in many respects, backward and under-developed countries. Why is this? Long before the white man came on the scene, your people, so to speak, had the chance—without the white race, to supposedly, hold you back—to develop and prosper. Obviously they, the nations of Africa missed their chance.

If you know you peoples past history, as well as the current history of the African nations, you must also know that not one of them has been able to establish themselves or achieve anything of significance, without the intrusion of the white man. Also, it should be noted, that those nations that have sought and received independence have, for the most part, gone downhill and for many, they could be considered basket cases in regard to their social ills. To attest to this one need only look at just a few of these nations, such as: Somalia, Rwanda, South Africa and just off our eastern coast—Haiti and, as well, Liberia.

The black leadership, in America, are quick to point out how many black slaves were killed by their owners and later by the Klu Klux Klan (KKK). What they are not quick to point out or seem unwilling to take note of is just how many are killed, by people of their own race. Black on black crime cannot go unnoticed or attended to. And, of course, your people must resolve this problem. You must accept it and deal with! Unlike your supposed leaders, you cannot blame everything on the whites. It is time for those in your community, who would stand up and face the facts, to obtain your support. Your present leadership—the schemers, the blamers and the race card players, must be called into question. For example: How is it that you're leadership of today are rich; while a great many of your people are still at the poverty level or below. Jesse Jackson has been on the scene for quite a while. He is rich. His children have prospered and become wealthy, while many of you have been left behind. Could it be that you are not only due for a change in leadership—you need it!

I do not see much being done by your leadership in trying to stop the inner city blacks from slaughtering each other. They seem to be ignoring this problem. Could it be that they can't make any money by attending to such matters! Just what are the concerns of the black leadership of today? It seems that blaming "Whitey" is their only answer to your problems.

It is, for me, hard to understand a race or group of citizens that, for well over a hundred years, have been freed from the bounds of slavery but remain unwilling to accept this fact. As

Robert Woodson once said, in essence: "it is about time you got rid of your plantation mentality."

Throughout my life, I have had the pleasure of being associated with many of our black citizens, both in the civilian as well the military communities. Many of them have become my personal friends and, as such, I appreciate and respect these relationships, I have always liked and respected them for who they are—not for what others would have me believe. There are a great many black leaders that are in effect, carrying the load in trying to maintain an objective point of view.

However and unfortunately, they are not given due recognition by their own people. Why? To me, it is obvious that their present leadership has been very effective in using a relic from the past calling them "Uncle Toms." Why do they do this, well they, the current black leadership know that if their message ever got out, they would soon become relics of the past, themselves.

What is their message, it is that they, these so-called Uncle Toms, choose to look at the entire racial situation in a balanced, realistic and fair-minded way. In short—they don't discriminate by race or color—they look at the facts and make their judgments accordingly. To all of you, and those of your persuasion, I have a heart felt appreciation for your efforts. For what you are doing to bring the races together and not trying to further divide us, I say thank you very much!

> "But the greatest menace to our civilization today, is the conflict between the giant organized systems of self-righteousness—each system only too delighted to find that the other is wicked— each only too glad that the sins give it the pretext for still deeper hatred and animosity." Herbert Butterfield.

Chapter XVII

Two Faces—Two Faced

In his book The Making of a President published in 1964, Theodore H. White wrote the following:

> "...One cannot speak, therefore, of a single Negro Community in a big city. Each has two Negro communities: one that is beginning to achieve. And the other that is threatened with the collapse of all human values, all dignity, all functions; they are almost as different as two separate ethnic groups."

This statement is as true today as it was back in the Sixties. Mr. White, in his book, further states:

> "...What is a man's relationship to, and responsibility for, his fellow man? But one must mark for future historians that, long before the major candidates began this discussion, the Negroes of the black ghettos had raised the matter in blood and made it central on the American agenda of the next generation."

He goes on in this book to point out and characterize the riots of 1964:

> "...The riots of the summer of 1964 were not race riots. They were worse: they were anarchy, a revolt led by wild youth against authority, against discipline, against the orderly government..."

A common characteristic of the riots was a senseless attack on all constituted authority without purpose or objectives. While in the cities racial tensions were a contributing factor, none of the nine occurrences was a "race riot"...In almost every case the riots began in the same manner; a police episode...a police arrest, and than a boiling over of a mob against the police..."

If the outlined prelude to a riot seems all too familiar—it should!

In his column "...The left's war on Police, by Nicholas Stix and published in the Middle American News, he states: "...The first shots in the war on America's mostly white urban police began in the 1960s. That's when the New Left—which combined communism with racism to create today's multiculturalism—charged that the police were an "occupying army" in the nation's urban slums, as if those neighborhoods were foreign nations..."

Comments as above, in essence, became a declaration of war on our men in blue.

The war on the Police continues to this day. Throughout our country, many blacks of this nation, particularly in their leadership, are making every effort to handcuff our police officers. Without an effective police force, the entire nation will be put at risk. To further their objective, they have come up with a new one: RACIAL PROFILING. Once again by redefining words, to their advantage, they are slowly but surly further encumbering law enforcement in the exercise of their duties. It is no longer their goal to disarm our lawful citizens but, as well, to incapacitate our police officers ability to protect us. I am left to wonder just what is their goal? What I do know is that an unarmed citizen in the climate of today, would be a citizen at risk.

In those nations where they have allowed the politicians to disarm them, crime has dramatically increased. One might ask, in our nation, why is it that blacks commit most of their crimes on their own people. We all know that "Hating Whitey," for many blacks, is a reality. If this were so, one would have to believe that their crimes would be directed at the whites as opposed to, on their own people. The reason, I can only surmise, is they know that the whites are, for personal and home protection, better armed.

At present, this factor of an armed citizenship, so to speak, kept the wolves at bay. Looking to the future, I can only see a further expansion of crime. We have, over the pat 30 years or so, thanks to liberalism and the "PC" crowd, created a belief in many of today's children that they are owed a living and if they don't get it—they will take it. While this nation, increasingly, becomes a High-Tech society, our High-School drop out rates seems to be growing, or at least, remain constant. Consequently they will not be able to compete for the high paying jobs. As such, they will either become totally dependant on the Taxpayers for support or turn to a life of Crime. This will, in my opinion, all to soon come to be. At such time, who among us would choose to remain or become disarmed? Only a fool!

Today, instead of looking to this problem, the black leaders are concentrating on Affirmative action to get the partially qualified of their citizens—those that are to a degree educationally limited—into our colleges. You would think that the education of all their children would be high on their agenda.

Instead, they are more concerned, for who knows why, that a few are, because of the color of their skin, given "Bonus" points to get in ahead of other, fully qualified students. This is, to say the least—wrong way thinking! However, I believe the education factor is not as important to them as the in-your-face politics of the matter. How could any reasonable person not come to know that the grater good would come from the education of all their children?

Today, all to many of our underprivileged children are forced to remain on the educational ship US TITANIC by their own leadership, as well as some of their parents—destined to go down with the ship. To my black friends, you wanted equal rights—you got them—now you must apply your liberties that will benefit the greatest number of your children. Do not be swayed by the politicians. YOUR LEADERSHIP IS LETTING YOUR CHILDREN DOWN—and for what—personal gain! Do not let them enslave your children to a life of dependency. They, your children, are the future of your people—do not let them be used! Used by those who would seek to benefit from their ignorance! You must demand that they be given a lifeboat—a SCHOOL VOUCHER!

By the way, these towers of knowledge and influence are introducing Rap into the educational system—our public schools. What next—Ebonics! I just know that our corporations will be waiting with open arms to greet these Graduates. Folks it's not Rap, it is a "Bad Rap" to hang on your children!

Today, the profiteers within your race are out for themselves. Do you think that Reparations is for the good of your people? These cheap shot profiteers, from time to time and in all races, are selling your people a bill of goods. Reparations will profit no one. It will only serve to draw our citizens into a confrontation that will serve no one any good. However it could have Drastic Consequence—consequence to our people as well as our nation. Together, we must look to the future. Only in this manner can we all be enriched. It is no longer a question of overcoming, it is a matter of enduring!

> "When the occasions present themselves, in which the interests of the people are at variance with their inclinations, it is the duty of the persons whom they have appointed to be the guardians of those interests, to withstand the temporary delusion in order to give them time and opportunity for more cool and sedate reflection."
> Alexander Hamilton.

James J. Dobranich, Sr.

Closing Comments

There are many reasons why it can be flatly stated that the decedents of former slaves should not only be denied any form or reparations, it is to be demanded, by all right thinking people, regardless of race, creed or color, that such a claim by one group of our citizens on another be soundly rejected. Unless it is, not only will the people become entwined in a bitter struggle, the entire fabric of our nation will be torn to shreds. The division of our people, in such a cause, will only evoke bitter hatred between the races. No one would profit—we will all lose.

Abraham Lincoln had it right: "A house divided cannot stand." Over the past thirty years or so, many blacks have found the freedom they have sought and richly deserve. It is only now to be Lost and squandered away, only to enrich the greedy among you? I ask you, should anyone, black or white, now come to the forfront and attempt to profit at your expense?

To enrich these "Vagabond Profiteers," at your expense, would be nothing less than a national Tragedy! In my humble opinion, by giving your countenance to such an endeavor, you would become complicit in what can only be described as an attempt to "Pick the Pockets" of your fellow countrymen. In so doing, you would destroy everything you have gained. In this manner—you will not have OVERCOME, but only SUCCUMB to personal greed, at the least, and at the most an innate hatred of the white race. There can be no other explanation!.

THINK BEFORE YOU ACT FOR TO ACT BEFORE DOING SO MAY HAVE CATHOSPHIC CONSEQUENCES

James J. Dobranich, Sr.

Reference

Africa and Africans—By Paul Bohannan and Phillip Curtain
Africa in History—By Basil Davidson
America's 30 years War—By Balint Vazsonyi
At any Cost—By Bill Sammon
Hating Whitey—By David Horowitz
Markets and Minorities—By Thomas Sowell
The...Book of Presidents - By Wyatt Blalssingame
The making of the President, I964—By Theodore White
The Negro in the Making of America—By Benjamin Quarles
The New American—By Michael Barone
The Family under Siege—By George Grant
The SEVEN MYTHS OF GUN CONTROL—BY Richard Poe
The story of the Gun—By Ian Hogg
Race and Culture—By Thomas Sowell
Readings in American History—(edited)—By Robert C. Cotner,
    John S. Ezell and Gilbert C. Fite
When Nations Die—By Jim Nelson Black

Also:
The Random house Encyclopedia (electronic edition)
New York Times Almanac's
The Readers Digest
A self-published book: "United We Stand by Diversity we Fall" -
    By James J. Dobranich Sr.
Webster's Pocket book of Quotations Dictionary/

James J. Dobranich, Sr.

James J. Dobranich, Sr.

Reparations

James J. Dobranich, Sr.

James J. Dobranich, Sr.

James J. Dobranich, Sr.

About the Author

After Joining the United States Air Force, in 1948, the Author, after an honorable career, retired in 1968. Upon retirement he moved with his wife and five children to Texas, where he still lives.

During his years, prior to final retirement except for a short time, he worked as an Insurance Agent, retiring from same in the year 1985. With his final retirement in 1992, he took a course in writing and eventually worked for a local paper as a weekly columnist. After writing for the paper for several years, he started work on his first Novel. In 1999, he self published his first completed work: Divided we Stand by Diversity we fall.

The Book "Reparations" is a personal repudiation, by the author, of those who claim to have a right to financial compensation based on America's involvement in slavery.